Whack me when I swear

Author & Illustrator
Enoch Hartwell

Dedicated to:
Kora, Malachi, Ezra,
two more special guys Adam and Elijah
along with somebody else's kid

Edited by smart people

Outskirts Press, Inc.
Denver, Colorado

The opinions expressed in this manuscript are solely the opinions of the author and do not represent the opinions or thoughts of the publisher. The author has represented and warranted full ownership and/or legal right to publish all the materials in this book.

Whack me when I swear
All Rights Reserved.
Copyright © 2011 Enoch Hartwell
V3.0

This book may not be reproduced, transmitted, or stored in whole or in part by any means, including graphic, electronic, or mechanical without the express written consent of the publisher except in the case of brief quotations embodied in critical articles and reviews.

Outskirts Press, Inc.
http://www.outskirtspress.com

ISBN: 978-1-4327-7207-9

Outskirts Press and the "OP" logo are trademarks belonging to Outskirts Press, Inc.

PRINTED IN THE UNITED STATES OF AMERICA

Thank You:

The Great I Am
My wonderful wife Nancy, Kora, Mom&Dad,
Gram Clark, two awesome brothers
Rindo (you're a blast)
Dawn (you're a sweetheart)
Bob Hanson
Pastor Dave, Pastor Willie and Pastor Ken
Bruce & Ann Johnson, Mark & Amy Farkas,
Joe & Betty Hopkins, Eric "Sumner Drum Guns"
S.C.H.O.C., Sunshine Farms, Ralph Tutela
A few in law enforcement:
Don Fontaine, Don Coons, Andy Hart,
Doug Hackett, Matt Foss and Will Nielson
(Glad we never wrestled gentlemen)
Thanx again John Dean
(I owe you some apologizes)
Adam
(you should be in here)
Not to mention
all those in the stories who made it possible.
One more group I sincerely hope we all thank continually:
Our Troops
"THE AN NAZ BOYZ"
Nate MacLean
and all the others who have been wounded in the line of duty.
You people are heroes!

Disclaimer:

All stories in this book are true to my knowledge and/or memory. Either names have been changed, or only first names have been used so as not to offend any of the persons discussed. You can try to sue me, but there are thirty-two thousand Daves and four-hundred and thirty-two thousand Johns on this planet....

All views and opinions in this book are one sided and mine. I'm not psychologically schooled and don't expect you to start a religion based on "Whack me when I swear." This book is solely for reading purposes and killing time.

Just because I was shooting an AK-47 in the state in which I live doesn't necessarily mean the state of your residence allows the same. In other words, you need to find out the laws of the state in which you live before attempting anything discussed in this book.

If you are in any sort of violation of laws in any state or country, don't call me. I'm not a lawyer either.

Index:

Chapters:	Pages:
Myself	1-5
You	6-13
Parents	14-20
Step Parents	21-24
Friends	25-31
Girlfriend/Boyfriend	32-36
Sex	37-40
Teachers/Probation Officers	41-46
Drugs	47-57
Cops	58-63
Jail/Juvenile Hall	64-68
America	69-75
Life in General	76-85
Food for thought	86-88
God	89-100

Forward:

Wow. Hey, thanks for checking out this book. I hope it helps make some kind of sense out of a few things, or at least a couple of good decisions, a little on down the road of life.

Growing up, I never really had a good role model. **Role Model def**: Someone who can relate to you and the things you go through. Someone who has "been there-done that" so-to-speak and has a few decent opinions. Someone who could give a little heads up about what might be around the next corner in a way you can understand it.

This book has a few things to say to someone looking for answers and wanting that little heads up.

These days, as I drive through the streets, I see kids everywhere that remind me of me when I was a teenager. The only skateboard I ever owned had metal wheels. If I was a few years younger, I'd be on one now... Believe that.

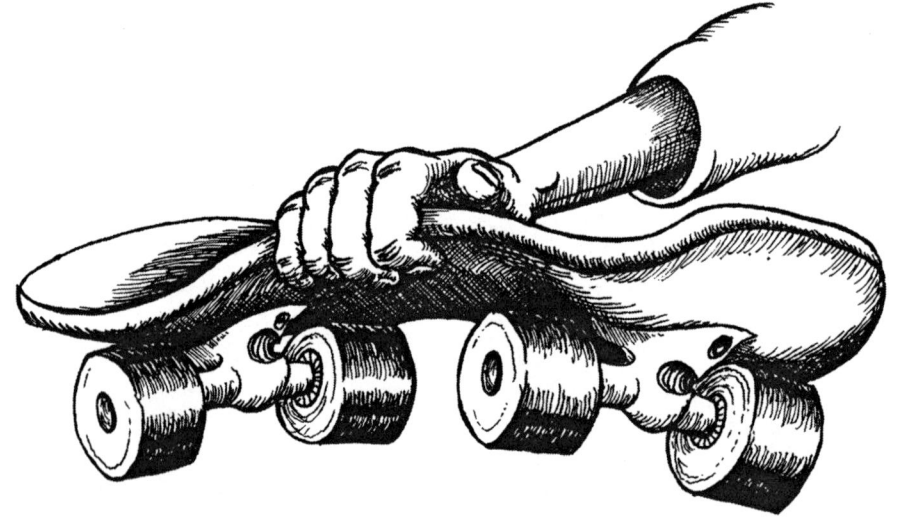

In my day it was jean jackets with a heavy metal patch stitched on the back, long hair, boom-box and high top sneakers. If you had all this equipment it was fair to say you weren't playing by all the rules, at least that's what it meant in my case.

I learned a thing or two over the years and have had my share of ups and downs. This book is full of stuff I wish I knew then. (If I had, I'm sure I'd be in a different place today.) I urge you to continue and press on. I know it can always get better. (The choice will be yours.)

I've had a few people come to me over the years, talking about killing themselves. For sure it's a tough life, but we all have what it takes to overcome even if it seems like the end of the rope is near. I also believe that life can be won no matter the state you're in now, because you never know what's behind door number two. I heard a guy say one time, "You can always get back to where you were, and then go higher." I believe it, but I also believe and know from experience: where you want to be isn't always that far away. Tomorrow is a new day and no one knows what it will bring.

Hopefully this book will give you the kick in the pants we all need once in a while to get up over that hill. Its purpose is to pick your butt up off the ground and help you go higher. I wrote it for fellow humans who are going through the same one time life as me and who don't mind a decent value and a wise decision every now and again.

I hope you enjoy reading and I'll always encourage you to write (anything), just write.

MYSELF

Unfortunately, I'm not talking to you and listening to where you're coming from or what you've been through. All I can do is tell you where I've been, what I've done and a few things I learned along the way.

My name is Enoch, like E-knock (on the door). The name may sound cool with e-mail and all the e-stuff on the internet, but trust me, third grade in nineteen seventy-eight... it wasn't. Punks used to call me "E-snot" and a whole list of other words. Many times people ask me for my name again because they don't think they heard me right. So I repeat myself and then add "call me anything but late for dinner"... which (so I've been told) "Isn't cool," but I do it just the same. A lot of my friends call me E, which is what my parents called me growing up and I can live with that.

I came along the month after Jimi (Hendrix that is) died. It's a shame (not that I was born) that Jimi died. I've always digg'd burning guitars, castles made of sand and a good old Hendrix tune.

I was actually born to hippies, if that's what you call people who live in the middle of the woods without running water or electricity and haven't seen a pair of scissors in ten years. I've seen the pictures of me running naked with the chickens, which I guess was ok in the early seventies if you lived on top of a mountain without neighbors for a couple miles. Dad had to get a phone line put in for my mother after a couple of years because she grew up a city girl and wasn't coping so well without some kind of communication with the outside world. We lived there until I was almost four before we moved into civilization. Not to say that we became civilized, just that we finally had civilized neighbors and

someone to talk to other than our (long-haired) selves.

I have two brothers. Both from broken homes. I am the middle child or was the middle child until I grew up (which is still in question).

Not sure it had anything to do with being born in the wild, but in my younger years I always seemed to find the trouble. You could follow the busted street lights to my house. I wasn't too good in school, couldn't see the darn chalkboard and was too "tough" to tell anyone. I didn't really go to high school much at all. I was what you might call "Tardy". When I did go to school, I was the class clown. Growing up I had sibling rivalries, alcohol problems, car wrecks, wasn't too good with cops, did B&E's (breaking and entering), got into drugs, more cops, dealt guns, had girlfriends, went to all the parties, more alcohol, more cops, had fights, more drugs, fights with cops and of course more cops... which led to court hearings. What comes after court hearings? Money, time, time, and money. (If you're wasting either of these as I did, you're going backwards.)

   I never thought I'd live past twenty-three and I say that because one night my friends and I were asking each other how long we thought we'd make it. I couldn't get my brain past twenty-three. I was sixteen at the time, about twenty-four years ago. It was also about the time I sat in the back row of the church with AC/DC cranking in my headphones. One time an usher (a guy in a suit) came back and asked me to turn it down, it was bothering people in the front row. I was one of those baaad kids. When you hear, "He's out of control," that was me. Needless to say, church didn't last much longer for me.

   I inherited some drawing abilities and when I was eighteen years old a buddy talked me into getting a tattoo machine.

Armed with all that, created a new kind of monster for sure. I inked people for about seven years. It didn't make for a very good lifestyle, if one can only imagine. I was basically living like there was no tomorrow, itching to get high, jumping from girl to girl, and drunk all the time.

I was reckless and thoughtless for a long time and now I'm paying. Paying with what? With the knowledge that if I had taken a different approach to life then... How Now-Brown Cow!! I could be ruling the world! Ha Ha Haaa!!. Hey! I can believe that and why not? Besides someone has to rule the world and I honestly don't think any one person is better than the next- class, race, religion, color or any other whatever for that matter. I'm trying to be an optimist (which is good by the way.)

As I've gone through life, I've gathered regrets by the bucket. If you haven't, you will... trust me. The longer you live the more buckets you'll fill, but it doesn't make you a screw-up and it doesn't mean you're an idiot either. It does however show indication that there's the possibility you're human. One thing I have determined and I wish I'd done a lot earlier, is to minimize the buckets I fill by trying to make the right moves, do the right things and not be so thoughtless and careless about what tomorrow might bring.

Having met enough people, I do believe I'm normal. I'm not real sure who defines normal, but when I look in the mirror I tell him, "you're as normal as normal gets."

We can all agree, the boxer doesn't win any belts or cash prizes laying on the canvas. So I'm going to get up and if I go down again... I'll get back up, because I want to win this thing. I can and I will, because I've made the decision to be

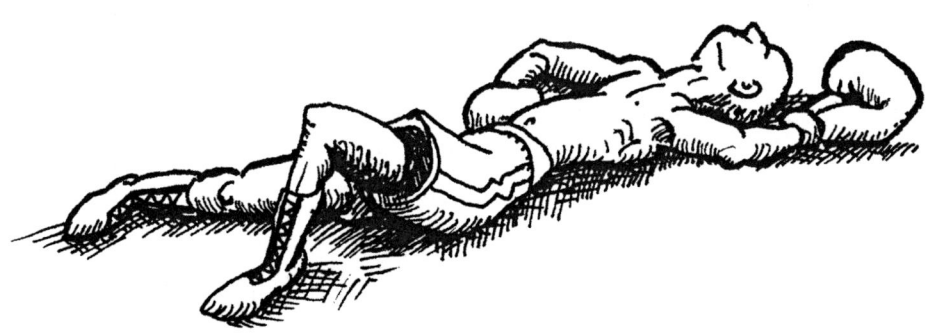

a fighter. It's a choice that each one of us can make and I believe it! Make the choice to be a fighter!

YOU

Let me tell you a few things about you. Now you may be thinking, "You don't know about me!" Well read and see. First of all, I can say in complete fairness that you are not perfect... or are you? (If you are, I can't argue with geniuses, but you're in for a whole new set of problems-I'm sure.)

You are you and there will never be anyone like you... not ever! There are things about you that no one knows, like how you feel, what you believe and certainly what you think about different things... No one can get into your head. You have feelings and thoughts that make you who you are. "Feelings!" Yeah it's a mushy word huh? Not really though because anger and hatred are feelings also.

Note: Feelings can wreak havoc on one's life if not dealt with and controlled. Be careful because feelings are not always right and acting on them can sometimes get you into serious trouble. Always try to take some time and clear your head before acting on your feelings. (Time is the tell all.)

You're a mix... I'm a mix, everyone is a mix. All through life, people have influenced and affected who you are and will continue to do so as long as you live. Unfortunately, some of those people are not the best fighters and so we should try not to get mixed up with people who lie around on the canvas. Notice I said "try". Sometimes that's a tough one and it's why I say try and say try again. If you try-try again, more often than not, you will eventually get it right. So if you find yourself getting wrapped up with people who drag you down, make a point to wean yourself off of them, or just drop them all together. Then watch out who you pal with in the future. You've heard it said, "You can't judge a book by its cover," but you can judge a tree by its fruit. Be careful you don't hang on bad trees and eat the fruit thereby.

All through this life people affect us and (believe it or not) you affect them. Yes you do! Things you say and do influence people's lives. I remember seeing something on the news awhile back, it's an extreme example but something to think about and be aware of non-the-less. A girl had a problem with another girl at school. I can't exactly remember where, but anyways, one found the other on My-Space, created a false identity and started e-mailing her. The identity she fabricated was that of a boy. After a while the girl started to confide in the "boy", unloading her problems on him and accepting what he said as someone who really cared. He shared similar problems and solutions with her and eventually he told her she should just kill herself... She did. True story, sick story! But I shared it to show just how much one can influence another and sometimes very quickly. Now I'll quote something my mother used to say: "Believe half of what you see and none of what you hear" Seems to fit here with internet profiles, not to mention most of what you watch on television.

We've all heard, "Sticks and stones will break my bones but names will never hurt me." Well, that's not true if used as a statement. That saying was actually a confession of someone trying to be strong, but if you are the one calling names, you may be hurting someone and perhaps very badly... not good I promise. The Good Book says, "Do unto others as you would have them do unto you." Why? Well for one, it may help you live longer.

One way or another you have an effect, but it is never that you don't matter. Trust me, you do matter. If you say or do the right thing to build someone else up rather than tear them down, you could have a friend that would walk on coals and go through the fire for you.

You also have gifts and capabilities, talents and ideas. You may not think so, but you do. Maybe it's just that you haven't discovered them yet? (Dig deep.) As for myself, I discovered things as I went through time. (Remember? Time is the tell all.)

I'm sure that when George Washington was still crapping his pants he wasn't thinking he was going to be the first president of the greatest nation on earth. I'm sure the thought wasn't racing through his parents' minds either, especially after he hacked-down their cherry tree.

I happen to believe that you're a person that could go places and do great things if you put your mind to it. Now, I'm not trying to puff you up, I'm trying to get you to think about something... You can do it! Tell yourself, "You can do it!" Come on, say it. (Look over your shoulder and make sure no one sees, because you don't want to look stupid.) Even if it's just under your breath, say "You can do it!" You may say, "That's stupid!" Ok, fine. But you're the one that has to live with yourself and pay the prices later for the choices you make today, tomorrow, the next day and so on.

Or, you actually did say under your breath, "You can do it." Good for you! Now your question is, "Do what?" Answer: Whatever it is you put yourself to do.

You are responsible for your own actions. Now, this one may be a little tough to chew on, so I'll give a small example: Either you broke the window or you didn't! No one threw the rock for you, and if the police come, usually the witnesses will describe the one who threw the rock, not the people standing around watching. Ultimately, you can say you didn't do it and you may have people fooled. But, if the truth is you did do it, you will have to live with yourself and I believe there will be a price to pay, regardless if you got caught or not.

Story: Years ago, three guys and I were building someone a house. The plumber was there and left an expensive right angle drill on the job. One of the guys said to me, "I want to take that drill." I said "Go ahead... and it will be one of the most cursed tools you own." He looked puzzled and asked, "Why, because of the serial numbers?" "No," I said, "because it was obtained wrongfully. So on your way home, when the motor in your car blows, don't wonder why."

Needless to say, he didn't take the drill. (Good for him.) Like the Good Book says, "You reap what you sow." I believe it! Many people try to have double standards, they rob and steal and then wonder why nothing goes right in their lives. Hello!??

I visited a local jail for ten years and talked to guys about life. A number of my friends knew I was doing this and one day one of them said to me, "I feel bad for those guys, because some of them are innocent." I said "No Jack (that was his name), they're all innocent. Ask any one of them." I've seen so many people in jail, convicted of a crime you know they committed and still professing to be innocent and/or blaming someone else. I often wondered why they just couldn't accept the fact that they messed up and deal with the consequence.

I can tell you that if you want to play the blame game, chances are pretty good you will end up in more trouble later and maybe even for the same thing. It definitely takes a bigger person to accept the responsibility for things they did... it's a choice. Say it, "I'm Bigger!" Clear up the situation and quit working on filling the next bucket of regret. It will go better for you in the long run. If you have been playing the blame game, knock it off! Start accepting the responsibilities. It may not sound like fun, but being productive isn't always a blast. Ask anyone who's driving a BMW with the kick'n system and the sweet rims.

I believe very strongly that everyone (yes even you) has brilliant ideas and marvelous dreams that, if acted upon, would put them over the top.

Make no mistake, I'm not advertising organized crime here. But when it comes to your dreams and ideas, I believe we must use the rules of the Mafia... "Don't tell no-body!" or at least tell only those you can trust. It's not necessarily that they'll steal them from you, but most people's visions have been shot to death and

many times (probably most times) by their closest "friends". "Ayh, that won't work. That's the stupidest thing I've ever heard." If you hear that enough times you'll drop the ball for sure.

You listen to Eminem? He talks about struggles and opposition. "But I kept tryin'." He knew he was onto something. He didn't care what other people thought. He used persistence and eventually he made something out of it. I'm not necessarily talking about rapping for a living either. I'm just saying you can make it if you persist. It's not any different for him than it would be for you when it comes to going after your dreams or goals. It's really not! You can! Most dreams don't happen overnight either... I say most, like 99% of them.

I once heard Walt Disney went to over 200 banks before anyone would give him a loan for Disney World. Obviously, he battled some discouragement. Who doesn't have something that's got Disney on it? His determination and persistence paid off. We live in what's become a microwave world. Everyone wants it now. But reality isn't "what's behind door number one" (an old game show called Let's Make a Deal). In other words, not many people are actually going to have a million dollars handed to them. And hey, by the way, it's never too late either. Colonel Sanders was an old man when he got Kentucky Fried Chicken off the ground. PS: An old, white guy with a chicken business? Like the Good Book says "All things are possible to him who believes."

Hint: Be cool to the people you surround yourself with. (What goes around comes around.) Don't blame your friends and try not to lean on anyone too hard (they'll let you down). We're all human and prone to mistakes. If you want to win, you'll fight your own battles and accept responsibility for yourself.

You can lay down in front of a bus if you want, lean all over people also, but do either of these and you won't go too far. Stand up, get a hold of yourself, be a soldier and take what you want (I don't mean by force either). I mean by putting your mind to it and taking the time to accomplish your goal. PS: If you do take by force, there is a price to pay. You may not exactly know the price, but you won't like the end result I'm sure.

Think positive, be an optimist, because today is your day! What do I mean your day? Well you're still alive aren't you? You are you, so obviously, it's your day!

PARENTS

Almost a cuss word! **Def**: Big, dumb, lazy people with bad breath, bad haircuts, who (like Gestapo) torture with stupid rules, dumb jokes, slave-drive and are an embarrassment in public! If that's what you think.... You may be right. I'm sure my children thought that many times and I don't blame them.

We as parents... here's **my def**: Old, most of us have terrible haircuts, few have nice breath, none are perfect, been through a lot, seen people die, had things taken from us because we couldn't pay the bills, have things that plague us from our past, made many mistakes along the way, married the wrong people or they married us, been through our share of pets, had terrible parents who made stupid rules and the list goes on. Not only all that but your parents could have been the geeks at the lunch table no one wanted to eat with, picked on for their goofy shoes and coke bottle glasses.

You're the generation of cool and at this point your parents aren't supposed to be cool, they're supposed to be parents and we all know by now that they're the furthest thing from cool. So you can't expect them to suddenly chill out. The rule of thumb is parents are supposed to control with an iron fist. They're supposed to keep you on the straight and narrow. After all, if they're not trying, who is?

I will tell you this: my father was a pretty big dude. When you were messing up, he was someone to reckon with. I know what it's like to have my backside smashed up, which (believe it or not) I thank him for now. Can't imagine how much more trouble I'd have gotten into if I didn't also have to answer to him.

Parents don't know it all. It's been proven in court somewhere, I'm sure, and as a matter of fact, most of us don't even know Jack. You're the generation of computers. You could Google Jack and probably find out everything about him. Well put it this way, I'll bet you could go through school for just about anything and never leave your crib. You could learn everything from pulling teeth to rebuilding an F-16 jet fighter on the internet. (The f-16 thing may be classified information, but you know what I'm getting at.)

Collect yourself, close your eyes for a second and imagine life without computers and technology. [Moment of silence.] What would we do? Life would be slow! No cell phone, no i-pod, no Playstation, no computer, no myspace, no texting your bud quick-"whr u @??" Well, that was us... and anybody on earth before us. I know it's hard to imagine. I said that to say this... Parents can't fully understand where you're at because when they were your age they didn't have the technology and certainly not the same issues and pressures that go on these days. (Time is the change all and as long as it goes on, things change.) The world is totally different now, but don't use that as an excuse to throw yourself to the wolves. What I mean is don't have the attitude, "Well you never had it as bad as I have" or "you didn't have the problems I have to deal with" and fold up like a clam. (Clams live isolated lives, are eaten by about everything and nobody brings a clam home for mom to question.)

You only get one life. Ask yourselves, "Will I live or exist?"

Live Def: Wake up breathing, able to start a new day with chances and opportunities. Being able to attain dreams and goals (using persistence and determination). You are still you, a blood pumping, self-contained masterpiece with capabilities beyond imagination (if you stop and think about it).

Exist Def: To barely hang on. Good knot that's easy to hold onto, but it's at the end of the rope.

Hint: In many cases if you're cool with your parents, their attitudes will change.

Make a habit to put the trash out or something. Be a good room mate at least. Think about it this way: you eat the food, use the water, use the electricity, want rides here and there... whatever. That all costs money and we have all heard it a thousand times, "money doesn't grow on trees." Most of your parents go to work and deal with some jerk or a whole bunch of jerks all day, usually for eight hours, to feed and clothe you.

You might be thinking, "They don't go to work just to feed me." No, maybe not. But if you chow fifty dollars worth of grub in a week, take seven showers, watch twenty-five hours of electricity and drink fifteen gallons of gasoline, that means for at least three hours a day they dealt with a bunch of jerks and got migraine headaches to support your comfortableness. Be fair about it, think outside the box.

Ultimately if you want you can say, "screw my parents," and go to Juvie or Placement because that's what happens to a lot of kids when they kick against the goads. Like it or not parents are older than you (I didn't say smarter, I said older), which means they have had more time to become who they are. Make sense?

Bear with me on this one. Most parents would probably agree that when you were crapping diapers and were able to be picked up and placed behind the iron curtain of a playpen it was a whole lot easier than when you grew into a know-it-all eating machine with an attitude, who empties wallets, wreck cars and tries to control their lives-ultimately changing who they were. Some people (and I will say people because although you may not agree, your parents are in fact people) don't know how to deal with you. I'll repeat it more clearly. Many people don't know how to deal with their kids. It may not be that they don't want to, they just don't know how. I'm not making excuses for them, I just know that's the truth. Sometimes it seems easier, and maybe even seems safer, to send you to someone who can and does deal with kids/teenagers (people who have reached the height requirement for the Superman ride at Sixflags).

Maybe your thinking, "Hey, I can't deal with my parents." Well no one has a magic pill. That's why I wrote this chapter, to try to give you a different perspective on things, and ultimately to help you deal with each other.

There are many cases (unfortunately) where placement, or something like that, is all around better for the both of you. If that's the case, I'm sorry... but and a big **BUT** it is... don't let your rebellion and stubbornness be the reason you get locked up, because that could be a rocky road for no real reason at all. If you're doing your best abiding by the rules and things are tough all over, maybe you do need some help. I know there are many people who really want to help you and they can be found. Things can get better!

You are subject (by law) to your parents' authority until you are eighteen. Why should it be any different for you than it was for the rest of us? "Well I won't be pushed around," you say? Then don't be lazy, earn your keep and they'll probably quit pushing. If that's your attitude, be glad you weren't born a hundred years ago... four o'clock in the morning milk the cows, shoveling stuff 'til ten, go to school 'til one, walk home, eat (and it wasn't a box of Oreo cookies), feed the animals, shovel more stuff, milk the cows again, eat, do your homework, read for a few minutes, blow out the candle and go to sleep. Think I'm kiddin'? Lights weren't a switch on the wall and dinner wasn't a cell phone call for pizza delivery. Think about it for a minute [Moment of silence.] A lot of those families had ten kids and they had ten kids for a reason. Not to mention (back then) without DCYS and all the child welfare laws, a parent could just about pound the life out of a child and no one would say a thing to stop them.

Running away was a slim-to-none option either, because your friend's father would probably beat your backside and then bring you home anyway. Yeah, you could jump a train, but what then? Hunger would set in eventually and (back then) people looked down on vagrants, handouts weren't on every corner. If you would use your imagination for a minute, I think you would probably agree that most kids just did what they were told.

I know it's tough when you finally get to an age where you can compete with your parents. What I mean by that is when you (your intelligence and everything that goes with it) get to the point where you know (or think you know) what your parents know. I think it's when you realize how imperfect your parents are. There are some let downs and then some feelings like you must prove how imperfect and unknowing they really are. It might be over a period of years, but eventually you will find out that your parents don't really claim to be perfect. It's almost as if they pretended-and maybe they did so that you would listen to them and do what you were told. Then maybe feelings of betrayal come over you, like they haven't given you enough credit all those years. My gosh, they treated you like a child!?? Geeze, there might be a lawsuit there, but there's a big hole in your case... you were a child. As crazy as it may sound, you'll always be your parents' child. At nearly forty, I'm my parents child. **Webster's def:** #2 a son or daughter; #5 a descendant.

You should try to understand that it's difficult sometimes for parents to treat their children any different. After all, you have always been their child and it wasn't all that long ago you would have starved to death if they didn't manually put the spoon in your mouth. You can hold it against them if you want, but when or if you ever have children you will know better what I'm talking about. Here comes the airplane, open up the hanger... in goes the mashed up baby food and then WHAM, they spit it all over the place. You're kinda lucky you made it long enough to read this book. And when you think you're ready to make babies remember what you put your parents through, because the Good Book says, "As you meet it will be measured to you."

Anyway, as worthless as it seems, be a good little Johnny or a good little Suzy, so that later in life you won't regret where you have been or what you've done.

Hang in there, remember what we said about time? Deal with your parents. They won't be around long. Either you'll be old enough to get a job, move out and pay your own bills, or eventually they'll be pushing up daises. (The big dirt nap.)

STEPPARENTS

First of all, they can be very difficult to deal with.

My father and mother divorced when I was seventeen. Growing up, the thought of divorce never crossed my mind, I guess I thought they would stay together forever. Having been through it, I can say I don't think it matters how old you are when your parents divorce-it's never an easy thing.

They were single for many years, but eventually they both remarried. Now that I'm way old and don't have to live with these people, it's very easy to deal with my stepparents. (I can leave their house when I want.) However, if I did have to live with them, I'm sure things would be very different. Why? Because I'm not the one who married them and they would be someone brought into my life without invite. However, they are still stepparents and I have to live with the fact that mom/dad chose them to be their partners. It's only fair, you know?

You may have stepparents and let me tell you, as hard as they try, they will never be your parents. They're not supposed to be. They are, in fact, your mom/dad's mate. No kidding, right? I'll try to put this in perspective: Your mom/dad decided to get married again and now this person has moved into your house (or you guys have moved into their house) to be with their new spouse. They are adults and hopefully act like it. Your parent obviously loved this person enough to marry them, take up residence with them and I'm sure they trust them with you. If things aren't working out quite the way you think it should, you must understand that you are not their child. Bear with me, I'm not calling you a child, I'm using the word as terminology.

You see, it may not be easy for either one of you to deal with the other and that is perfectly normal. I say in good faith that they will try to help your parent with you as best they know how. However, they may not know how and they may be very uncomfortable doing so, even if they have their own kids. It's probably as awkward for them as it is for you. I'm sure that some things they do and say rub you the wrong way and may even make you down right mad. Remember, in relationships it's always a two-way street. In other words, things you do and say may rub them the wrong way also.

I believe the best way to look at a stepparent is to look at them as older roommates... they are. As a roommate, there should be a certain amount of respect for each other in the dwelling. You should think about something else: they may cook your food, give you rides and pay bills, which means that they are pulling more weight and are more responsible for the household than you are. Which in turn means that they are actually providing for you and because of it, you have become somewhat subject to them. I believe most stepparents do their best in dealing with the kids of their new spouse. You must remember that they will never treat you like your parent does, you're not their child. In turn, usually you will not treat them like your parent, although you should respect them even if you don't particularly enjoy their company.

Unfortunately, a lot of kids just plain don't like their stepparents- this is normal. It may seem as though they are trying to fill your parents shoes and it may be that they are trying to fill their shoes, which cannot be done... of course. I do believe that common ground can be found and stepparents and kids can get along beautifully.

If you're having a hard time with your stepparent, maybe you should try to talk to them about it and maybe even let them know what bothers you. Reminding you the Good Book says, "Words fitly spoken are like apples of gold in settings of silver." This could mean using a careful approach (everyone has feelings), in other words try to be nice about it. Maybe you could even ask them to read this chapter from your new book. There are many things that can be touchy subjects and we really want the outcome to be a good one, not one that ends in another fight.

If you don't realize this, I'll bring it to your attention: fights between you and your stepparent may mean fights between mom/dad and your stepparent or even with mom/dad and yourself, which usually means more trouble and headaches. I didn't say that to burden you with their relationship, it's not your deal, ultimately it's theirs. They are the ones who got married. However, respecting your mom/dad is going to mean respecting your stepparent also. Remember you only have to deal with it for a while, because soon you will be able to move out and start a life of your own. Then you can be like me and leave whenever you want. Until then, I'm sure things will go a whole lot smoother for you if you respect them. In most cases stepparents are out of your control. Hopefully they're not out of control, but if they are, do your best to keep it to yourself.

Smile, you only have _____ months left.
                Fill in the blank

FRIENDS

If you can count your friends on one hand you're doing good. I heard that one time and liked it. I find a certain amount of truth in it.

Friend Def: Someone sent from we don't know where, or even why, to cry on us, spill their guts, repeat the same stories and stupid jokes day after day, sometimes even hour after grueling hour. One who also teaches us how to wipe our backsides properly (as if for umpteen years we weren't doing it right). One who doesn't even know jack until you're absolutely positive about something and then somehow they become a conflicting Einstein Jr., letting you know just how wrong you really are.

The fact is people usually hang with someone because of the benefits. "What? I don't have anything." Ok, so you're broke, no car, no guy/girl (couldn't get one if you tried) so they look good crackin' jokes about your sorry butt. Get away from 'em. They're not your friends. You're nobody's sorry butt. You just don't belong in that crowd. If the future could be seen, you wouldn't want to be any part of them anyways! Out of ten, two of them will end up in prison, three will be pill junkies, two will die in car wrecks, the rest of them will go no where as fast as they can.... use your imagination and don't let it happen to you.

If you shoot hoops and you stink like me, then they play with you because they beat you all the time-making them look good. Oh!? you're good at hoops? So they'll play to compete. If you beat them, they have practiced and so in turn you were a benefit to them. Try not playing and see if you're still cool with those guys

You know the crazy part? Some of your parents are your best friends, you just don't know it yet. They're still the worthless losers nobody wants to hang with and I can understand where you're coming from-I thought that for quite some time. Didn't make me a bad guy. We all have a right to our views and opinions. In this country we can even voice them.

My parents were uncool for a long time, until I took off on my own and watched my friends wither away. My parents were the only ones concerned enough to stick around and help. Not only that, but when you move out and have a hard time paying rent some month, usually mom/dad will give you a hand just so they can keep their house to themselves. Just kidding, but they will help you when no one else at all is to be found.

Anyway, be careful who you're calling friends. It could cost you in the end and trust me on this one-they won't be around to help you pay, especially if the payment means a little time in jail.

Story: On the fourth of July when I was eighteen, a "friend" (I'll call him Skip) and I had gone to a party. We had a few drinks, lit off some fire works and then went to a different party. The second party was at a guys house who lived out in the woods. We stayed there longer than the first one and drank keg-beer until we were ready to leave. We got into a Chevy, El Camino. For weeks he'd been raving about the 350 motor coming out of a race car and I guess at that point it was time to show the stuff. While he was revving the engine up real good, a few guys lifted the bumper and the back tires came off the ground. Right before the thing was ready to blow rods though the hood, they let go of the bumper and the tires about burned up before we shot down the road. With his foot right to the floor, a couple of miles and about three gallons of gas later there was a truck at a stop sign ready to make a left turn. We sailed by, sliding sideways and burning the tires around the corner.

Up the hill we went, picking up speed quickly. Skip wasn't letting off the gas, so I thought maybe the truck was trying to catch us. I looked back to see what was going on and way back at the stop sign the truck was still sitting there, but I could see blue lights in the trees. I turned back around and said, "Cops". He didn't even acknowledge me, but kept the petal to the metal. A few seconds later, trying to use better judgment I said, "Pull over." He said nothing, just looked real determined to out run the cop. A couple more seconds went by and I said again, "Pull over!" This time, he glanced over and said, "I ain't got a license."

Well by this time we were flying down the road, a sign flashed by and I realized where we were. I put one hand on the roof, one on the dashboard and yelled "We aren't going to make this corner." Finally he came to some kind of sense and let off the gas, by then we were going over one-hundred miles an hour for sure. The corner wasn't all that bad, but at that speed and the fact that the car's suspension was junk it was more than bad, it was terrible. When we hit the little swell in the beginning of the corner, we sailed across the road instantly. His arms were flying around the wheel and he managed to keep it in the dirt on the other side of the road.

For a fraction of a second I looked straight down the road on the other side of the corner. I thought for one split instant, "He made it!" but because he had the wheels cranked around so bad trying to hold the dirt that when the car caught the tar again we were shot like a bullet across someone's front lawn and then into the trees. The thing that saved us was a boulder we'd hit halfway across the lawn, flipping the car like a corkscrew and sending it squeaking between the huge pine trees and landing on the driver's side. We hit the boulder so hard, the transmission was coming through the firewall. The steering wheel looked like a half moon used by the passenger. The windshield was one big spiderweb and the rear bumper was found a hundred feet from the car.

I remember the initial impact and can still hear the wreckage. I think it was the G-force of the flip that blacked me out. I opened my eyes to darkness, totally disoriented and curled up in ball. Fear for my friend's life came to my mind as I regained my bearings. I said, "Skip". Again this time a little louder, "Skip". There was no answer. Horrified at the silence, I yelled, "Skip!" Then I heard the muffled groan, "Get off me". I was piled up right on top of him. Relieved at the sound I climbed up and out the passenger side window and jumped to the ground. I stood for a second, anticipating Skip to follow. "Hey," I hollered and, "Hey!" again. Skip half yelled-half groaned, "Rock the car, my arm is stuck!"

I started to push on the accordion (which used to be the hood). Finally he came up and out the window, jumped to the ground and went limping off into the woods holding his arm. That's when the pain hit me. It felt like someone had shoved a crow-bar right through my chest and out the backside of me. Then I smelled gas real bad, so I started to get away from the car, when I heard, "Stop! Stop!!" I looked back toward the voice and could see the cop in the headlights of his cruiser.

I tripped over some roots and he came running over, screaming, "Are you crazy?" (something I've heard way too many times). I laid there until paramedics arrived. That was the first and only ride in an ambulance I ever had. One night of alcohol and "friends" has cost me for twenty years. Some mornings I have to roll over and lay on my back for a few minutes before I can actually get out of bed. Skip never got caught. Was it all worth him getting away with not having a license? No, it wasn't!

The Good Book says: "Iron sharpens iron, so a man sharpens the countenance of his friend."

So if your "friends" are actually bringing you down (or maybe even trying to kill you) you should seek different company. Sometimes no company at all, is the way to go. So if your one of those "Loners" without any friends, you may want to consider yourself fortunate... seriously!

Scenario: The two coolest kids in school are talking trash about someone else and it appears they want you to get involved in the conversation. You know who they're talking about and it would be easy to join right in because the person they're talking about isn't that bright anyways. But if you do join the slashing, the two cool ones will actually lose respect for you-if they had any in the first place. Why? Because if you would burn the not so bright one, chances are pretty good at some point you'll burn them to. Trust is like respect, it's earned. What goes around, comes around and if the people you hang with hack other people, at some point you'll be the target.

Story: A couple of years ago, I was at a friend's house. (She lived in an apartment complex.) Two guys that I knew drove into the parking lot, stopped and were talking to me from inside the car. One of my friend's neighbors (whom I didn't know) came out of his apartment and got something from his car. When the guys that I was talking to saw him, they started right in: "That guy is a scum-bag, what a loser..." On and on they went, sharing short stories with each other. Then they looked at me, clearly wanting me to agree and get in on the railing. I said, "Hey, whatever it is you guys got against him, is what you got against him. He's never done anything to me. I don't even know the guy and I've got nothing to do with it." They both looked a little shocked at my reply. But you know what? Both those guys know when it comes their turn for someone to start hacking on them, I won't be getting involved. That's the way it works!

Sometimes the best thing to do is to speak up and let people know you're a neutral party who's not getting involved with everyone else's back-bitting. It will make a statement. It may even protect the victim or could even gain one of those people who will go through fire for you. Sometimes people will be quick to jump in and join the railing when they don't even know the victim. Well, what does that say for them? Actions speak louder than words, you know? Hello! (Ignorance.) No one wants to be ignorant, do we?

Choose your friends wisely. Don't take unnecessary risks and if your gut doesn't like it, maybe it's not a good thing.

GIRLFRIEND/BOYFRIEND

Oh boy, I'm sure I'm going to say some stuff that's gonna rub some hairs. Ya know what I mean? I'll explain... animals are covered with hair that lies naturally one way. If you rub it backwards, they get ticked off. That's what I mean It might tick you off.

What is a girlfriend or a boyfriend? **Answer**: They are just that. Girl friends and boy friends, usually associated with some sort of intimacy. "Sex?" No! I said intimacy. **Webster's**: #2 a close, familiar and affectionate personal relationship.

Some people think it's someone they own and say things like my girlfriend, or my boyfriend.... No one owns me and I don't really want to own anyone. (Sounds like a Bob Dylan song!) Even married people don't own their spouse. They make a commitment, but there isn't any ownership. I'd rather have someone stick around because they wanted to, not because they were forced to. Relationships should be based on respect, a respect for one's own personal life. If you respect someone's life you will give them space to do what they want. After all, isn't that what you expect? By the way guys, when it comes to girls-respect isn't something you demand, it's earned. Respect isn't gained forcefully. Force reaps fear (usually ending in disaster) and respect has to do with honor.

Webster's respect: #3 esteem; admiration; #4 proper acceptance or courtesy; #8 to refrain from intruding upon or interfering with.

Webster's honor: #2 a source of credit or distinction; #3 high respect, as for worth, merit, or rank.

Girls, you won't get respect dressing like a hooker. Guys will follow you around like ducklings, but don't expect them to respect your life. Won't happen!!

Listen to reason: People do what they want. What happens if they are forced to the contrary? They get uptight, build walls, resentment, rebel and the list goes on. If you are trying to force someone to see it your way, it will go bad and in the end, maybe even explosive. There are many different ways people try to force others to see it their way. Many people manipulate to control, it may sound something like this "If you love me..." or using a guilt trip like, "I waited for you to call all night, if I knew you weren't going to call I would have done such and such..." when in fact you never said "Wait for my call." Even if you did, why would they bring it up? ...to use the guilt trip method. If they can get you to feel guilty, chances are the next time you will call-but not because you want to, but because you don't want to have to deal with their attitude later. What is that? Trying to force you to do what they want you to do.

Whether you're a guy or girl, you are you with a life and in this country it's a free life. Let them live how they want, you don't want anyone controlling you, do you? Be strong and let them do as they please. If they don't want what you want, let them go. Trust me, it will be better for you in the long run. "Yeah, who's thinking about the long run?" I can tell you, not the stupid kids in the paper this morning. Girl gets hit on at work, tells the boyfriend who's in jail. Then the boyfriend gets two of his friends to murder the guy. Guess what. All go to prison (even the girl)! Now what? Mom can't help you there.

Don't be fooled. As spiders weave webs they get stronger. You may be getting caught up in something you'll seriously regret later. If you're already in a bad relationship, be careful. Get out, get help, find support. It is there, you can find it and there are people who will help you! Don't live in fear. The choice is yours. If the shoe doesn't fit, don't wear it. "Why?" Because you'll get blisters, unless for some strange reason you like blisters?? If the gears grind-don't try, because you'll blow up the machine. Girl, if you don't feel good with all the questions, get out. Chances are it will get worse. Dude if you don't like her hangin' with other guys, move on. Obviously that's what she does. Snip it. It could get ugly. Protect yourselves.

Based on a true story: Tom meets a girl named Jenny in the twelfth grade. They become friends and as time goes by, they become quite close. The only problem Jenny has with Tom is that he is a bit jealous about her talking with other guys. Tom is head over heels for Jenny. Anyways, some more time goes by, one thing leads to another (Tom smooths her with words) and they start to have sex. Months later school is out, both graduate and they move into an apartment together.

After a while, Jenny is becoming unhappy because they are having a hard time paying bills and Tom is a slob. She starts to confront him about his living habits and respect for her (the roommate).

Jenny gets out of work at three-thirty and she's home by four, but after a while she starts getting in at five-thirty or six. Tom asks what she's been doing and Jenny tells him she has been hanging out with her friend Sarah. Tom doesn't believe her, so Tom starts showing up at Jenny's work around three-thirty. The first day, Tom tells her that he just wants to do something with her today. The next day it's, "Oh, hey, I was just in the area." Tom manages to foil plans between Jenny and Sarah, because Tom doesn't trust her.

Jenny is getting sick and tired of going home to a pig-sty and a boyfriend sitting

in front of the X-Box. Not much changes over the next few months, except that Jenny just discovered she is pregnant. By now these two just about can't stand each other. Jenny's fed up with Tom's questions and controlling personality. Tom is sick and tired of Jenny's nagging and complaining, and certainly doesn't trust her at all.

Jenny's friends all tell her to leave him and the girl at Tom's work is telling him how much she likes him.

Question: How much longer do they last? **Answer:** There is no correct answer, because they could last forever and be totally miserable for the rest of their lives or they could end it tomorrow with a child stuck in the middle. If the story sounds like it's yours, you will have to answer it for yourself. If it doesn't sound like yours, make sure it never does.

This story happens everyday in America and you're not immune if you have sex with a girlfriend/boyfriend.

Life does go on, use your head.

SEX

First of all, most of your parents can't (or think they can't) talk about it anywhere near you. I remember when I was about twelve, my father caught me with a pack of matches (thankful we never burned anyone's house to the ground). On the cover of the

matchbook
it said, "I know everything I need to know about sex." my father saw that and his forehead crinkled up, he snatched them from me and with the utmost disgust he said, "You don't need anything like that." The funny thing is he wasn't concerned with the matches, he just didn't like what it said on the cover. You might say, "That's dumb" and maybe these days it would be, but back then nobody said hell or ass on the television, they didn't play Slipknot on the radio and nobody was killing Kenny. The thing was, he didn't know what to say or how to deal with the topic of sex with his kid. Looking back, I kinda laugh because if I knew all I needed to know about sex, things wouldn't have been so rough for me later in life. All in all, Dad should have just patted me on the

back and said, "That's right son, way to go boy. Run along and start a blaze with your pals."

   I believe a few things about sex that may or may not be anything you have heard before, but I will share them with you non-the-less. First of all, I think that when you have sex with someone you give away something that can never be taken back. So you give something away and what if you guys split up tomorrow? I also believe that ultimately it should be shared with one individual and only one individual for life. Unfortunately, that doesn't seem to be the way the ratings go on public television. To be honest about it, I haven't exactly stuck to those beliefs, **BUT** I haven't always had them. Since it wasn't a golden rule for me I have paid dearly and continue to pay, as do millions of people around the globe for one reason or another. A huge reason would be disease, of course. I'm sure you have been told about the various nasties involved, so we won't get into them. If you don't know about them, that's a good thing. If you must know I'm sure you have a health teacher or someone close that will share all the information with you. By the way diseases are everywhere and can be caught instantly!

   Another huge reason one may pay dearly for sex would be pregnancy, which means children of course. It's a very serious situation that will, in fact and as a matter of fact... very factually, change your life **forever**. No joke! Not a joke! Very seriously a forever situation, well forever as far as your life and the child's is concerned. Again, health class has more answers. Think before you act.

   Girls: Now let me tell you something you may not be aware of, but should be. I've heard guys laugh and say, "Yeah, I had a virgin once" and then something like "she followed me around forever" like it's a joke. Many girls' hearts have been broken because they believed what the guy said, like the love he has for her and how he wants to be with her forever, blah, blah, blah. The truth is, if he loves you that much, he'll stick around a while before he makes all kinds of moves on you. Guys will tell you anything to get what they want. Don't be fooled.

Guys: The quicker she's willing and the better she is at it = the more the practice. In other words, she didn't learn that from a fortune cookie and she probably won't stick around long. Smarten up for a minute, listen to reason... Your heart will get broken and you will be tormented in ways that suck. Keep your head on straight. Don't put all your energy into a relationship. Life is short and there's much to be accomplished first (If you want to be successful). Be strong and abstain so that when the right one comes along, you won't have to battle a closet full of skeletons. I've witnessed many bad endings... young people who basically hate each other and a baby in the middle of the whole mess.

Listen, life is real, it's not a game... we can't take things back- especially children. Sex not only makes babies, it also weaves webs-many times (probably all the time) with people you don't even know that well. A huge number of relationships basically start out in a bedroom before they find out if they even like each other.

Guys/girls one more thing: don't have kids for your parents to raise. They had to raise you, you can't expect them to raise their grandchildren. Kids are supposed to visit Grammy's, not live there.

Again, it's a responsibility thing. Accept it, deal with it. Don't be a slouch.

If you're in a situation and there is a child involved, stay strong and fight for your rights. I don't mean physically either. Let the laws do the ruling. Definitely exercise your rights as a parent because a child needs both parents. A mother can't do and give what a father can and vice-versa. Again, there is help if you look for it.

Think before you act. Consequences can be very painful.

TEACHER/PROBATION OFFICER

I'm quite sure teachers and probation officers would get along beautifully. They have a lot in common. Here's why I say this: First, they both have report cards to fill out, call it like they see it and (if need be) they have to bring down the hammer- so to speak. Both teachers and probation officers want to see you pass, believe it or not. Trust me, neither of them go to bed and dream up ways to nail you to the wall. They deal with way too many people to pick you out of the crowd. So unless you've given them some major reason,

it's not happening. If it is happening and if you can't find any reason why they would do such a thing, it's not against the law to talk to them and ask for specifics.

If you're getting hammered on, chances are it maybe because you run your mouth too much or you're disruptive. It's got to be something that you're either doing or not doing that is causing you all this anguish.

Most teachers are in the profession because they like to teach and work with kids. I know this because my father was a teacher for many years. Forty years later, he still talks about some of his students and experiences in the classroom. I can definitely tell you, they're not in it for the money because the pay isn't all that great-neither is it for a probation officer. So if it isn't loaded with benefits, why else? I believe a sense of accomplishment and worth and helping people better themselves has a certain amount of satisfaction for a lot of folks.

If a teacher had a classroom full of "A" students, I'm sure he/she would feel pretty darn good. Same for a probation officer. If all the people in their caseload were doing good and on the straight and narrow, they would place their heads happily on the pillow at night. I know this is true, because on graduation night they're usually smiling when they hand out diplomas and patting people on the backs.

Both (in most cases) will let you slide once, twice and sometimes over and over again. But they have a job to do and if your sliding all the time, then you're not learning and they aren't doing their jobs properly. Then they're forced to bring down the hammer. They have a boss too, you know.

Ok, so you still say they wake up in the morning, a light bulb comes on and they think, "I'm going to pound on so and so today."? No, they don't! They don't even want to hear from you or see you-only when they have to. They want you to be a success, it makes them look better when everything runs smooth and they're turning out model citizens.

Story: One year, my dad had a student that was constantly disrupting class and just wouldn't quit. Finally, one day he called the student into the hallway. When the student stepped into the hallway, my dad shut the door behind him. Then he grabbed the kid by the shirt collar with both hands, took him off his feet, smashed him up against the lockers and told him, "I've had enough of your crap. Now you'll go back in there, sit down and keep your mouth shut." Dad never had another problem with him. Years ago I met that kid, he's the one that told me that story. He actually respected my dad and told me he was one of the best teachers he'd ever had. By the way, that "kid" is like ten years older than me-this happened in the sixties.

When I asked my dad about it, he told me he always felt bad about doing it. Knowing my dad pretty good, it wasn't that he disliked this guy. He actually spoke pretty highly of Tommy, he just wasn't the kind of person to put up with too much "foolishness". I think he just snapped because he'd had enough. If you ever try to teach a bunch of people, you will find out how hard it is when someone is being disrespectful and disruptive. It's hard, it's frustrating and it makes you feel like you're wasting time.

These days if a teacher did that to a kid they might go to jail, but they would definitely lose their job. I told you that story because I was hoping you would get an idea of what a teacher may feel like doing when you refuse to be cool and keep your mouth to yourself.

Teachers and probation officers are human. Eventually they'll snap and it won't be good if it's you they snapped on. Why go through all that? Because, believe it or not, you're only taking yourself down. Hey everybody!! We have to fend for ourselves. I don't know about you, but I'm sick of going backwards.

Your teacher/probation officer deals with three hundred and thirty-three idiots in one day. All they want to do is make it through without a situation. They have a job to do, I'm sure it's stressful enough. Their handbook doesn't explain how to deal with long-haired, jean-jacket- wearing punks who do nothing but draw on books all day and pay absolutely no attention to anything.

Short Story: The police brought me back to school for the second time in a week, so the principal took me into the hall and said, "Look, you're out of here. If you want to come back to school, bring your parents." He'd had enough of my attitude. I took it as "Hey vacation!" So every morning I got up, got dressed and went to my friend's house. Finally one day I walked in the door and my mother asked, "How was school today?" I said, "Fine." Then she flipped her lid and started yelling, "You're a liar! The principal called me today and said you haven't been there in two weeks!" I was busted and then had a whole new set of problems.

I just wish I could go back and do it all over because school really isn't that hard. The hardest part about school is dealing with everyone, but I guarantee even that wouldn't be so difficult if you're not trying to be the most notorious kid in school. I would bet it would go so much easier if you kept to yourself, with your mouth closed and took the class a little more seriously.

If I'd applied myself I would have aced all my classes and became the honor roll student Yale was begging for. Instead, I really wasn't trying to see any light at the end of the tunnel and because I was being insubordinate and rebellious the train ran me down-so to speak.

Twenty years ago seems like yesterday, so ultimately it all got me nowhere in the speed of light.

Because of my choices then, I pay now. "Pay with what?" With the knowledge that if I had made different decisions... I could be working on brains, sporting a big house on the ocean, cruising a sweet ride, with vacations off the coast of Aruba. Instead I sawzall walls, breath insulation and struggle to pay my light bill.

It really is what we make it. The Good Book says, "You reap what you sow" I heard one fella say it this way, "We pave the road we walk on." How true it is!

DRUGS

Here's another subject that may be hard for parents to talk about. Some people are able and qualified to discuss this topic, however many don't have a clue how to go about it. So, while you are still reading this, I'll drop a few of my experiences and opinions on the matter.

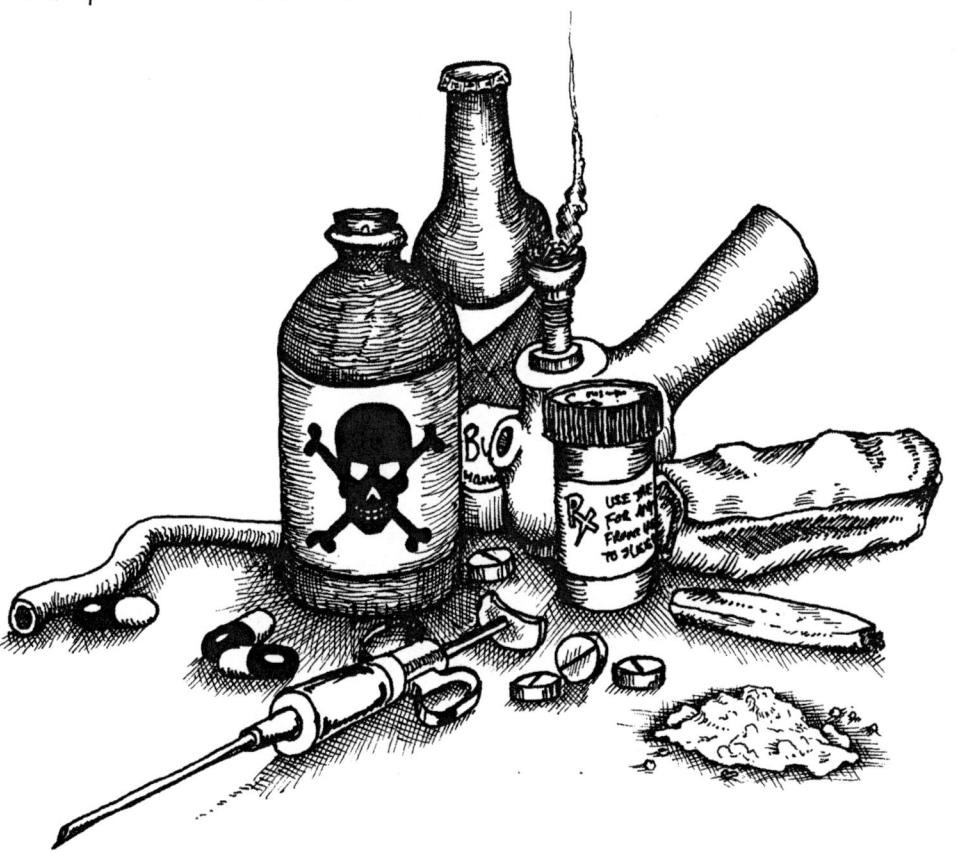

I started using drugs at the age of sixteen, alcohol and pot (marijuana) for starters. Not too much later-mushrooms, cocaine, LSD, a small number of pills and eventually crack cocaine. I feel as though I'm one of those quite qualified to discuss the issues and problems with drugs along with the effects it has on one's life.

In my younger years I never agreed with the old saying, "Pot leads to worse drugs," but that statement has proven itself in my life and here is why. The people who smoke pot are illegal drug users (like it or not). Illegal drug users purchase drugs from illegal drug dealers... obviously. Check this out: Supermarkets sell food. Hamburger is food. On your way through the supermarket (for hamburger) you might stumble into some cookies... get it? Not only that, but after a while hamburger doesn't do it for you (you'll want something different) one desires a change now and again.

People get high for the feelings. After a while, they'll usually look for (sometimes are simply introduced to) something that creates different feelings. I know I did and I also know many others who did the same. Argue it if you like but my mind is made up, having "been there, done that."

I don't use drugs anymore and will share some reasons why.
First of all, drugs separate me from reality, which seriously slows down production. I have also been jailed a couple times due to drugs. They have cost me serious money (drugs themselves, lawyers fees and court costs). I've seen people's lives completely destroyed by using drugs, not to mention spending every dime they make on them. Drugs definitely rule lives in more ways than one!

Story: I had a carpentry business for over five years and had up to five employees at a time. Over the years I acquired a job trailer and many tools, ladders and what-nots to get the jobs done. One day a guy that was working for me asked, "How did you get all these tools?" I pointed across the room and replied, "See that nail gun?" He answered, "Yeah" Then I said, "While you were buying a bag of weed, I was buying that nail gun." It may sound kind of crude, but it was kind of

a dumb question, don't you think? Some people need "in your face" theology. Why waste a bunch of time? Did he get it and start buying tools? No, he didn't! He later went to jail because of drugs and when he got out, violated probation (with drugs) and went back to jail. He got out again, not too long after that and went back to jail. That was ten years ago and last I knew (like a month ago) he is back in jail. Why... is he stupid? Not necessarily. He just got the ball rolling and once the ball is rolling, it's not always easy to stop it. My suggestion: Don't get the ball rolling, but if it is, stop it now because it only picks up speed until it hits the bottom. It may not be easy to stop, but there is always help if you look for it.

My opinion: Drugs of any sort, whether it's over-the-counter or under-the-table, have negative effects on people. It may calm nerves at the time but, there will be side effects, both mentally and physically.

Alcohol Def: A liquid which, when consumed, creates idiots who blah, blah, blah about absolutely nothing, turns eyeballs in stain glass windows, spins brains like merry-go-rounds, causes unknown things to happen with unknown people and the results may also be unknown... possibilities are endless and much too often cruel.

Story: I woke up one morning and couldn't open my eyes. I had to literally peel my eyelids open because they were all crusted together. As I rubbed the crusties from my eyes and peeled one of them open, I saw gray... I was looking at a gray... brick wall. Realizing (at the same time) how hard the object was that I was rolling off from and had just slept on, It quickly dawned on me that I was in a small jail cell. Then came the sore wrists, lump on the head and the bruised ribs. I couldn't for the life of me remember how or what could have landed me in such a predicament. I shuffled over to the small sink near the iron door and began to rinse off my eyelids. That's when the fire started... in my eyes that is... then my face... neck and forehead began to burn. Mace reactivates with water you know. Ok so, about a week later I bumped into this guy and the first thing he said to me was, "Youurrr crrazy!" When they say it like that, it's because they know something.

Assuming it had to do with the arrest, I asked him what happened. It was a question I had asked before, because once you "black out" more will follow... honest. (Blackout is a term used by alcoholics when they wake up in the morning and can't remember the previous night.) Usually when one finally finds out what happened, all they want to do is crawl under a rock, at least for me that was many the case. Anyways He was amazed I couldn't remember, apparently he never had that problem but this is what he told me... "You and I were walking downtown the other night, bumped into each other and started carrying on a conversation. I could tell you'd had a few beers, but you didn't seem too bad. As we were walking along the cops drove by... out of nowhere, you leaped off the curb and yelled... (he put his arms up, motioned his hands in a way one does guiding a truck to back up) raised his voice and hollered, "Come on suckers."

That will definitely get you there and was absolutely nothing I would have done sober. Lucky for me, no charges were filed because it could have been a whole lot worse. Assaulting police officers is a serious offense. That story might sound crazy or even funny, but when you're on alcohol in excess, you won't make good decisions. Many lives have been ruined and even lost (in an instant) because of alcohol. As soon as one starts to drink, they give control of life to something else. Don't let it happen to you!

Marijuana Def: A plant that, when smoked or consumed, creates numbness, empties wallets, creates "friends" who mooch like gigantic leeches and brains that lie dormant like a frog in the mud during the winter months. I've heard (a number of times), "Since I quit dealing, no one stops by anymore." Gee, good friends?

Cocaine Def: A powder that, when sniffed, creates nerves that stand on end, jawbones that float as if not attached, shreds wallets/bank accounts and everything worth anything and creates monsters who want for more and will even search carpets sometimes until daybreak.

Story: I once heard that cocaine affects a valve in the heart and every time you use it there is a fifty fifty chance of the valve closing and not opening again-resulting in death. Then like three years ago, a few teen-aged kids were using cocaine one town away. For one of the boys it was the first time and his heart stopped, killing him. His friend panicked (not knowing what to do), brought him (his body) to the hospital and dumped him out on the front lawn. The friend was later arrested and brought up on charges. I never knew them, but I always felt bad for their parents.

Heroine Def: Usually starts with pill addiction, causes honest, hard- working citizens to rob grandmothers, steal from children, lie about everything and anything, shreds dollar bills down to the dime and creates a sickness beyond one's control.

Story: One particular job I had while I was operating business, was a new roof on a two-story building. We were putting down new plywood which involved ripping off the old rotted wood and using nail guns to fasten it on. After nailing the plywood on, we would cover it with some real sticky stuff that came in rolls, three feet wide and seventy-five feet long. We would roll it out as long as we needed, then cut it off and peel the paper backing off so we could stick it to the plywood. At one point I asked one of the guys (I'll call him Tom) to go down and get something from the truck. He stood up and started across the roof, then I heard a bang and something sliding. I stood up and looked over the ridge to see what was happening and watched Tom slide down the roof and disappear off the edge. He had stepped on some of the paper that had been removed and was laying around everywhere. Once he was out of sight, the air hose that was connected to the nail gun tightened quickly and the nail gun followed him off the roof. The hose wrapped around his leg on the way down. I scrambled down off the roof to see if he was alright. When I got to him, he was laying on the ground all curled up in the fetal position, trying to catch his breath. I looked him over for bones, blood and anything in obvious need of medical attention. After a few minutes he was able to breathe, sat up and removed his boot-his heal was solid black. The nail gun missed his head by inches. So fortunately, the only thing wrong with him was the bruised foot.

A couple of days later he confided in me. He told me that he had a bad heroin addiction and just minutes before his fall, he had used a needle in the garage to inject heroin into his arm. This was (to my knowledge) the first time I had any kind of dealing with heroin. I felt bad for this guy and he said he wanted help, but didn't know where to get it. Then another guy told me about a doctor that would see him and possibly give him the help he needed. I mentioned it to Tom. He said he would give it a try, so we made an appointment. When we arrived at the clinic, the doctor shook my hand, said he had heard about me (probably from some inmates in the local jail) and wanted to talk to me for a few minutes. We went into his office to sit down, Then he asked me what I knew about heroin. "Not much," I replied. So he began to tell me something like this: The first time someone uses heroin they'll get high as a kite. The next time they use it will take a little more of the drug to get high, but they won't get as high as they did the first time. Then as they use it they will have to do more and more, but the high will be less and less until they aren't getting high anymore at all.

This is what heroin does: It restricts the blood vessels, and arteries, while at the same time it slows the heart rate. When the effects of the drug begin to wear off, the heart rate goes back up, but before the blood vessels, and arteries return to their normal size. This causes great pain, usually noticed mostly in the legs-because legs have such big arteries running through them. The rest of the body also suffers due to all the veins running to all the organs and what not. This causes extreme nausea and vomiting. One way to ease the sickness is to do more heroin, either that or they will have to let the sickness run it's course (which I have seen and it ain't pretty).

After a while, people are using heroin to maintain and not to get high. It becomes a serious monkey-on-the-back, costs a lot of money and causes decent people to become horrendous liar's.

A great number of people who overdose on heroin usually do so by what addicts might call "chasing the dragon." After they use heroin for some time and stop getting high anymore, they will actually stop using in order to go through the sickness of withdrawal and then use as much as they were using before (hoping to get high again). However, their bodies have recovered from the drug enough so that it is now too much so they end up overdosing-resulting in death. Excuse me! No high is worth that kind of risk!

Back to the story: I had an empty apartment and decided to let Tom stay there until he got well because the doctor said he would probably sleep for a few days due to the medicine he was going to prescribe. We set up a bed, small refrigerator with yogurt and fruit and cleared a path to the bathroom. Then he basically slept for like three days. He was finally up and around and was ready to go back to work. It was just a few days later he was back into the drugs. Again, he confided in me and told me about his fight to stay away from the users and dealers that he knew. Again, he asked for help to withdraw and again I helped. This time though, I left to travel across the country and left another guy in charge of watching over him and doing whatever he could to help Tom. I guess he made it through again but when I returned, Tom was gone and so was about five-hundred dollars worth of tools. I never saw Tom again or my grandfather's hammer (which I guess I'm still trying to get over).

Pill story: In 2001 I was working on a roof. I stepped off the roof and onto a wooden ladder. When I shifted my weight over the ladder, the top rung broke. My left foot went crashing through three more rungs while my right foot was still on the roof, so when my body passed the edge I was flipped upside-down. I fell about twelve feet with my hand up protecting my head and when I hit the force plowed the palm of my hand into the ground, shattering the radial cuff against other bones in my wrist. The guys working with me brought me to the hospital right away. The first doctor I saw (not sure what planet he was from) said he was going to put the pieces back together. (Yeah, ok. By the looks of the x-ray, there was like sixty little fragments.) I'm not a doctor, but I have more sense than that, so I asked him if it would heal the way it was. He said he thought it would and so we opted for a cast instead of the expensive, unknown surgery. Anyway, on the way out of there he wrote me a prescription for fifteen Percocet, with one refill. It did help ease the aching for the first few days, but it wasn't long before I got the refill and when those were coming to an end someone gave me like five more.

To top it off, then another person heard about my injury and (trying to be helpful) brought a bottle of pills to my house. They opened my kitchen cabinet and put the bottle on the shelf and said, "Here, these are real strong. If you have any pain this will knock it right out." Before I got into bed, I remembered that and went to see exactly what they put in the cabinet. A whole bottle of OxyContin, about thirty or so pills. I knew a couple guys who were eating those things and they had been offered to me a number of times, but I had never taken any. This time, the thought crossed my mind, "Now is your chance to try one," but it was late and I didn't know what the pill would do to me, so I figured I'd sleep instead. I awoke in the morning, got dressed and rushed out the door. I picked up a guy on my way to work and as we continued the drive to work, I remembered the pills in my kitchen cabinet from the night before. Knowing what the pills were doing to people and that it was illegal for me to have them, I decided not to take the risk and to get rid of them as soon as I got home. As soon as I walked in the house that evening, I went straight to the cabinet, took the pill bottle into the bathroom, dumped out every one of them and FLLUUUSHSSSHHHSHSHSHH. I'm glad I did that! I never found out what they would have done to me and I never will.

I told that story because temptations come in many shapes and sizes, having them doesn't mean you're a terrible person. They can be overcome and it's a lot easier to resist them before you get into the stuff. Don't give in, be determined to win, stay strong and in the end it will be better for you.

I have watched pills destroy lives for years (literally rip lives apart), enslave people to work for more pills and turn decent people into scavenging animals. It's terrible. I find that most people eating the pills cannot be trusted, they lie like rugs and even to themselves. The best thing to do is... none! Be smart, don't start! If you already have that problem, come clean, admit it and find help. There are many people who know how to help you and they aren't even hard to find. You can be free again, if you take the steps. There's no better time than now.

All of the above: May land you behind bars, lose jobs, destroy bank accounts and/or anything you own, wreck families, hurt children, create undesirable so-called friends and the list goes way on.

   Well, there are a few of my views on drugs. They may show you a good time or two, but in the end they will hurt you more than it's worth. There are many clean ways to have a good time without all the side effects.

COPS

So you don't like cops? Oh, ok. So, you want to be a cop? I'm not talkin' to you, skip this chapter. Alright. I'll explain myself. I wouldn't want the job. I've had a hard enough time staying alive as it is and you're nuts, skip this chapter.

Now where was I? Oh yeah, you don't like cops. Ok, fine. You're entitled to your opinions but let me share my views on them. Let me make this clear, these are my views and I am entitled to have them.

Cop def: One hired by the community to protect people from rabid

dogs and shoot them if necessary. (Not everyone's running around with a handgun.) One who steps out into oncoming traffic and holds it back as long as it takes to get the chemsuit guys cleared for lift-off, so that no honest, hard working, taxpayer has his face burned off by terrorists. One whose daily duty is to physically chase, grab and wrestle down the naked man who has crapped himself and is now urinating all over the place, only to find out later he has eight known diseases and in the end wants to sue for

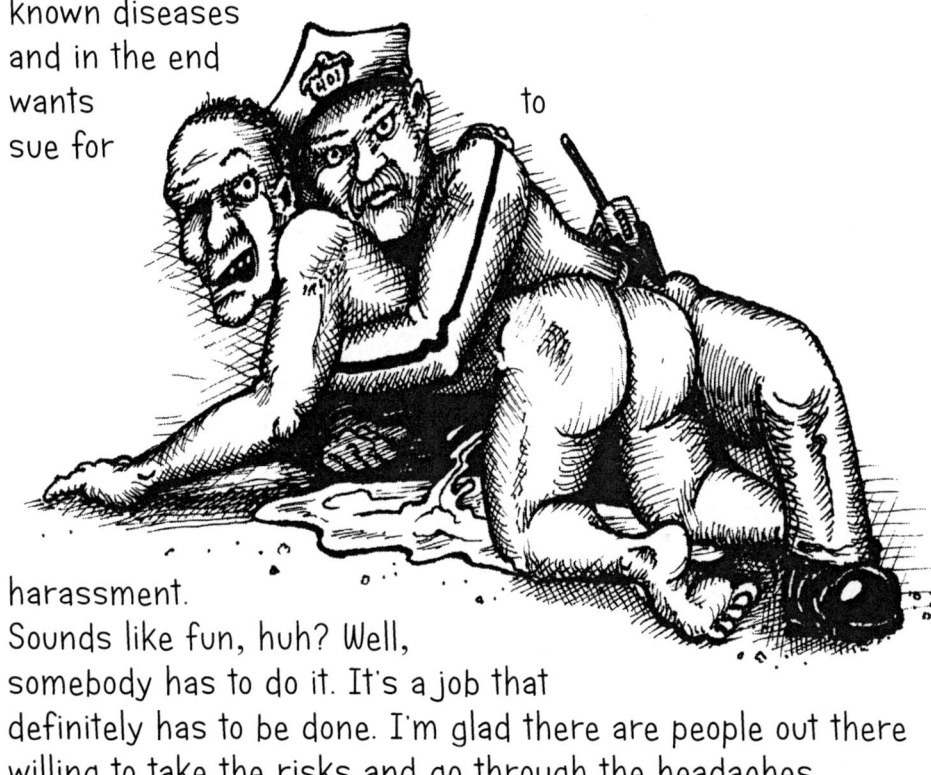

harassment.
Sounds like fun, huh? Well, somebody has to do it. It's a job that definitely has to be done. I'm glad there are people out there willing to take the risks and go through the headaches.

What I have found is that usually if you don't like cops, it's because you're breaking the laws they are hired to uphold. Trust me on this one... The cop isn't the one who hammers the speed limit sign into the side of the road. They also don't show up at parties without being called and the list goes on. They were actually hired by the officials of your community to do a job.

Let's try to put this in perspective: You work at the donut shop. Someone gives you an order and you've been hired to serve them what they asked for. The first customer steps up to the counter and asks, "Could I please have a large coffee, no sugar and two glazed donuts?" Instead you give them hot chocolate with whipped cream, a french cruller and seven packets of salt. **Question:** What happens next? **Answer:** They give it all back and say, "This isn't what I ordered." The next customer steps up and asks, "Could I please have a hot chocolate with whipped cream, a french cruller and seven packets of salt?" You give them a coffee, no sugar and two glazed donuts. **Question:** What happens? If you keep it up, eventually someone will tell your boss (the one who hired you) and if you don't smarten up, you'll get canned. It may be kind of a lame comparison but it's the same system. Cops have a boss also and if the boss keeps getting complaints about the way he is doing his job, eventually he to will get canned. So let me ask you: Why does the person at the donut shop try their best to give a customer what they ask for? **Answer:** He/she wants to keep their job. It's the same thing with the cop. They have a job to do-if they want to keep it.

Story: One time, many years ago, a friend and I brought an AK 47 assault rifle down to a sand pit, with a big box of ammunition. We loaded two thirty round clips and opened fire on some junk that was laying around, the main target was an old stove. We were pumping rounds into that thing like we were defending ourselves in a Vietnam rice paddy. It started sprinkling and after a while the droplets were landing on the barrel and hissing with little puffs of steam, so we gave it a break and got into the car to let it cool down. While we were sitting in the car, a cruiser pulled up along side of us. My friend, who was in the driver's seat, rolled the window

down to address the officer who was hanging out his window, looking like he wanted to communicate. The cop asked us what we were shooting for a weapon, my friend told him of course and then the officer said, "I thought so". He said he was sitting down the road listening to us for a few minutes before driving in and that he got a call from the nearby trailer park. The caller thought we were shooting automatic weapons I guess. "There's nothing I can do about it but I had to answer the call." he said, "I'll go tell her that everything is ok. Thanks guys and be safe," **Notice**: First, we were not breaking any New Hampshire laws. Second, he didn't draw a firearm and threaten to gun us down, he didn't call in five car back-up and no National Guard helicopters flew over with air support. He was doing his job: he answered a call from a concerned

citizen, which fit perfectly into his job description. Now if Dave (my friend) was hiding behind the stove and I was pounding it with heavy gunfire, the cop might have had a different approach when he pulled into the driveway- but Dave wasn't, I wasn't and he didn't. He simply was doing his job as best he knew how, as I'm sure most cops do.

Sometimes cops don't do it exactly right, after all where in the handbook does it say... When dealing with eighteen year old, long haired, machine gun toting stove shooters, one must...da,da,da,da... If it does say anything about that kind of situation, when exactly is he going to have time to read up on it? What I'm getting at is, being a police officer is (at times, I'm sure) a very complicated job with a lot of room for error (they call it the gray area). So chances are if something questionable wasn't going on you probably wouldn't have met the cop. Ok, ok. But if you weren't running your mouth at him when he did show up and just let him do his job, you probably wouldn't have wound up in the back of his car.

If by chance you did happen to be in the wrong place at the wrong time and were mistaken for someone else (which occasionally does happen) get a lawyer, take one on the chin and be more careful about where you play and/or who you hang with.

Hint: Fight them if you want. Let me tell how many will come... "As many as they need!"

JAIL/JUVENILE HALL

My buddy, Ralph, told me I should put something in here about incarceration and, believing he was right, I decided to toss my two cents out there. The first thing we'll do in this chapter is try to draw a mental picture of the topic.

Use your imagination to paint loneliness at its worst, along with open humiliation. You will be totally alone but there isn't any solitude or quietness involved and if you like any kind of personal space, forget about it. Privacy doesn't exists even when you use the bathroom... seriously! If you're not good at crapping with an audience, better get used to it. Shower shoes are a must and trust me it's not because you don't want to slip and fall (nasty). If you're an outdoors person, you are able to visit fresh air between one o'clock and two o'clock, in the fenced-in basketball court-unless of course it's raining or if they decide for some other weird reason your not going out.

If you like to come and go when you want or stay up late watching TV, none of this exists. If you like to pick up the phone and call people from time to time, you may-but only in between eight AM and eight PM and only at a serious expense to the one you're calling, because "collect" will be the first thing you say to the operator.

If you just can't stand the disgusting, nasty roommate you have, get used to it. If you are at all timid or a shy person, you will most certainly have trouble. It's not a requirement for inmates to be politically correct when it comes to your personality and/or emotional welfare. Many people are in jail for crimes against other people and many of these crimes involve serious infringements on personal space and/or property.

If you're the type of person who doesn't like people messing with your belongings, either you won't have anything or you will be seriously aggressive and willing to fight like a wolverine to keep what's yours. However, if you do this... you may be able to stay even longer because fighting is a crime you know?.

Well, who knows? Maybe you will learn to love the place like so many others who just can't stand to be away from all their new pals. After all, where else do you get three hots and a cot for free? As for me locked in a small room with other people I don't particularly care to be with... no thanx! No place to be as far as I'm concerned! Roommates outside of a cage are bad enough.

I really haven't experienced what it's like to actually live behind walls, thank God. The most time I've done is about two weeks total and only a few days at a time. However having gone into a jail for so many years visiting guys, I've seen the effects of being locked behind bars. Having been there, I do have a taste of what it's like not to be able to come and go as you wish. One thing that eats away at you for sure is not knowing what is going on with your friends and loved ones. Even if you do know, you're not able to visit them or do anything about it. I know at least one guy whose mother died while he was in jail and he wasn't even able to see her before she went. Life doesn't get put on hold because you're behind bars.

I've heard a thousand times, "Nobody comes to visit me" which is sad and you do find out who your true friends are when you're locked up. Nobody wants to go through a bunch of paper work, metal detectors and iron doors to have a short, monitored visit with a friend. It takes very strong feelings for

someone and an understanding of how important a visitor is to go through all that. I also know that the roommates you have in jail aren't anyone you would usually hang out with in your free time. After all, many of them are in there for some pretty nasty stuff and chances are real good that you wouldn't even have met them unless you went to jail in the first place.

Story: A friend of mine got DWI (driving while intoxicated) a number of times, until he finally had to go to prison for it. He wound up doing two years and said when he got there, they put him in a cell with a great big guy they called Chopper. After talking with other inmates over the first few days, he discovered how the man acquired the name. Apparently this guy was kinda slow and easy to pick on and his boss used to give him all kinds of crap until finally "Chopper" flipped out.

He ran over his boss with a truck, jumped from the truck, grabbed an ax from the back of it and commenced to chop him up... resulting in murder. He said Chopper never gave him a hard time but it was pretty freaky rooming with an ax murderer.

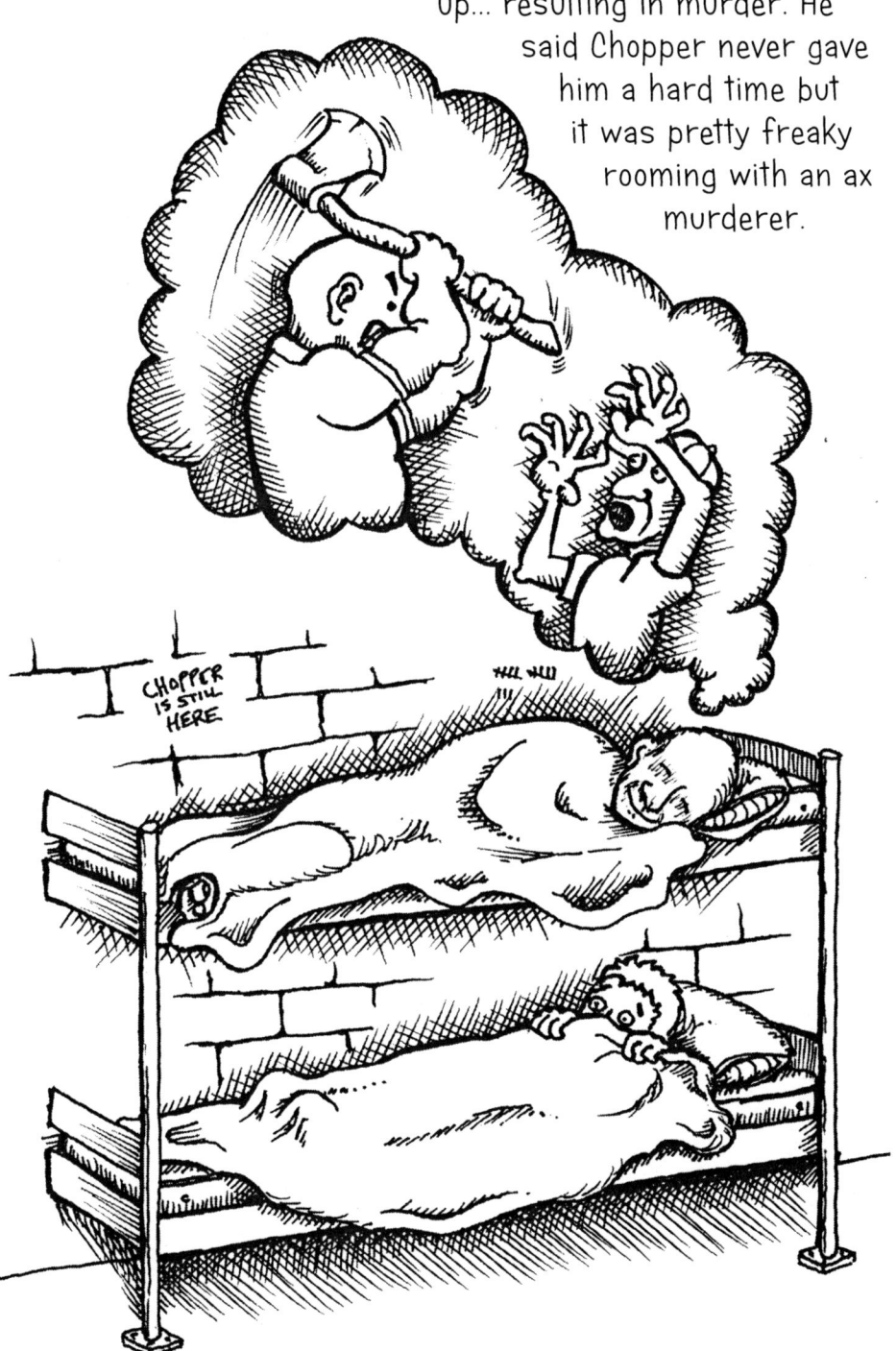

Finally on the topic: Did you know that the return rate for jail is eighty-eight percent? If you do the math, it means once you go to jail the odds are stacked against you... greatly!

Keep your nose clean so you won't have to go through the experience of the "Gray-Bar Motel". You won't miss out on life (because time waits for no one) and when it comes time to get a decent job you'll have as good a chance as the next guy.

AMERICA

Land of the free, home of the brave. What does that mean? Good question! Sometimes I wonder myself, however I do know some about American history and so I'm going to share a little bit to first give you an idea of how this country came about.

Our continent was seen by Columbus in 1492, right? "Fourteen hundred and ninety-two, Columbus sailed the ocean blue." He actually landed on islands near Cuba and on his way home sailing north, viewed the main continent through a looking glass. Then a man named Americo Vespucio was the first European man to put his foot on the continent in 1499 and the new land was named after him. Historians believe Columbus was wronged by not having the new land named after him, but what the heck really? We can't have two nations of Colombians.

Anyway, it was about another hundred years before people came from England and successfully settled in the new land. Jamestown, Virginia, was the first permanent settlement in 1607. In 1610 there was massive famine and out of five-hundred people only sixty-one survived by eating horses, dead Indians and some of their deceased friends.

Then twelve years later in 1622, on March 22, the Indians attacked, this time in the middle of the night, butchering three-hundred and forty-seven men, women and children "in almost the same instant." The settlers of this country had very few and short peaceful times. They continually battled winter, starvation, disease and Indians.

The French and Indian war broke out May 18 in 1756 and lasted about six years. Huge numbers of colonists were killed in probably the most vicious of all wars. Then a few years later on April 19 of 1775, the first blood of the revolution was shed as the colonists made a stand against tax oppressing England. This lasted almost ten years.

This country was built with much blood, sweat and tears over roughly one hundred and fifty years so that we could have the freedom to worship the way we want, choose our government and become what we dream to be. It's important that we know this and continue to stand strong for America and her values of freedom and liberty.

Story: Years ago in 1996, I worked at a shop reconditioning front end drive shafts. (You don't need to know the details about the job and you don't really want to know, trust me.) I was hired for the paint line and when I arrived they told me to go down through the shop, take a left and ask for a guy named Art. I found the right place and a guy who looked like Danny Devito came over to me, looked up at me and in a slow, very clear voice said, "Do you speak English?" It was the first and only time I had ever been asked that question in my life. In reply to him I said in a slow, very clear voice, "Yes and quite well if I might add." He threw his hands up and said, "Finally, somebody who can understand me." He promoted me to boss over the paint line immediately. I would like to think he could see smart all over me, but no, it was only because I spoke English. The place was crazy and, from what they told me, there were nine languages spoken in that shop. One night I showed up and a guy from the second shift (I worked third) said, "Man you should have seen it today! It was the Iranians against the Japanese." I guess an argument between two guys turned into an all out gang war at work.

It was crazy on the paint line as well. There was a Brazilian guy who spoke broken English and drank Vodka all day. There were two Mexicans, two Bosnians, an Albanian and one American right out of prison, who had just started, and another American named Frank, who looked like a washed-up biker. He always wore a baseball cap with a great big fish hook stuck in the brim and was prejudiced toward anyone who didn't speak English. One night, I could tell Frank was in a foul mood because he was constantly complaining under his breath.

Finally I heard him say, "Could you please move over?" A minute later he said it again louder, "Could you please move over?!" I looked up to see no one was moving and finally he said even louder (this time almost yelling), **"Could you please move over?!!"** He was talking to one of the Bosnians. I said, "Frank.." He cut me short and snapped, "I asked him nicely!" (I'm glad we aren't all that intelligent.) I said, "Frank, it doesn't matter how nice or how loud you ask him, he can't understand you." He said, "'Bleep, bleep' people ought to go back to their own country". Well, I had had about enough of him that night, so I asked him, "Frank, what nationality are you?". 'Huh?" he said. I repeated "What nationality are you?" With a puzzled look on his face, he said "Swedish."

Then I said to him, "Well, why don't you go back to Sweden?" There was a small pause, because he really didn't know what to say. Then I said, "You can't, can you? And I'll bet you don't even speak your own language." I should have given it a little thought before I said that, because that really ticked him off. Just a few minutes later he bounced his fist off the Bosnian's chin and they both got fired instantly. I really didn't think that was fair because the Bosnian guy didn't even do anything. His only crime was he couldn't understand Frank, and so I went with him into the office to testify to his innocence. However, there was no one in the office at the time who would listen to me or was able communicate with him. Between him and the other Bosnian (who turned out to be his father-in-law), they were able to ask me if I could go to his house so that his daughter could interpret what happened and then be able to

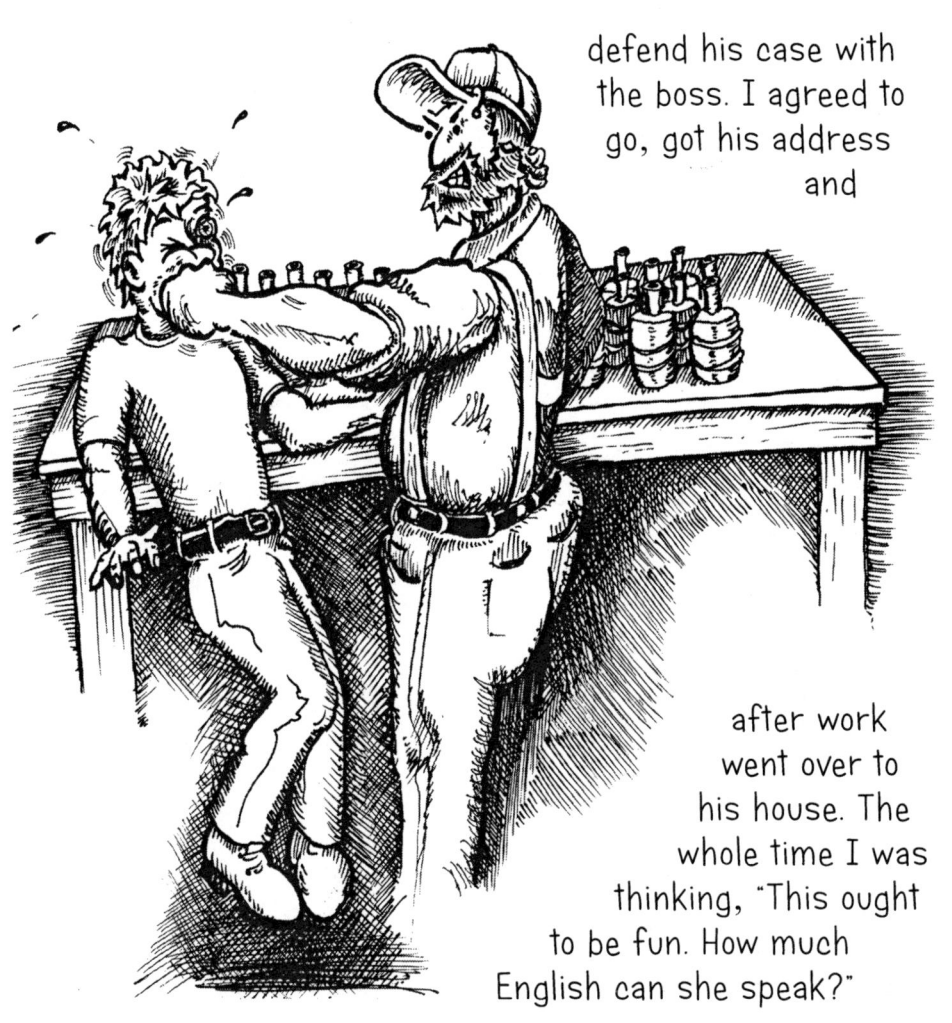

defend his case with the boss. I agreed to go, got his address and after work went over to his house. The whole time I was thinking, "This ought to be fun. How much English can she speak?"

So I arrived and when I knocked on the door Aberdeen (was his name) opened the door and was happy to see that I had come to his aid. He welcomed me in and went into a back room to wake his daughter. He really didn't look that old, so I was expecting this little girl to come out, to whom I would have to speak slow and clear... but instead out comes an eighteen year-old girl. She spoke English very well and, not to mention, like eight other languages. She actually worked for the government, placing immigrants in jobs and such.

I visited with them for half the day. She told me all about Bosnia and what kind of place it was when they lived there. They even showed me a video taken from a small plane as it was flying over the city. It was a quaint little city with a winding river running through it. She also pointed out how clean it was and the fact that there weren't many cars because most people rode bicycles. Then she told me how a group of Serbians came into the city and started killing people in the middle of the night. They stormed into common apartments and cut the throats of men, woman and children without any notice. She said there were piles of bodies in the streets and you couldn't even get a car through by the time they left Bosnia. Now imagine being woken up in the middle of the night by gunmen and your best friend (wife/husband) is murdered before your eyes before you have a chance to comprehend what's going on. Fathers, farmers, shoe makers, anyone old enough picked up an AK 47 and became the warriors and protectors of their own community. Aberdeen had two bullet holes in his leg to prove it.

That doesn't happen in the USA very often. As a matter of fact, it hasn't happened since you have been alive, it hasn't happened in my day or even our grandfather's time. No one alive has seen all-out war in our backyards, much less our own bedrooms. It's happening in many nations of the world today, but here in America we're not accustomed to fire-fights, bullets flying and hand grenades exploding in the streets. Why? This is America, that's why.

Now, how about this. You come up with an ingenious idea to power a city using a single sheep. In America it would make you rich instantly, but because you live in Russia, the government comes and takes your plans and ideas since you are only a common citizen that shouldn't have more than

anyone else does. Which was the way it went up until the mid seventies, because of a system called communism or socialism. That doesn't happen here because thousands of men have given their lives for a constitution to be set up which protects the freedom and liberties of each citizen of this country. I said all that to say this... Quit complaining about how bad you have it! There are literally millions of people (hello, on this earth) who don't even have refrigerators, much less anything to put in one.

I have grown to realize how good we have it here. I love America and, if need be, would defend her with my life.

LIFE IN GENERAL

As I go through time, I find little things or keys that I believe can help for a great life.

Question: What is really scary? I've asked a few people that question Usually this is what I get: "Ummm... I don't know... ahh??" Exactly! The unknown is the perfect answer.

Anxiety is a problem for a lot of people and I mention it because I believe it is

closely related to the unknown. So, I will share a view on the issue I think we all deal with.

Anxiety Def: Feelings of uneasiness caused by being held out a window by an ankle, forty floors off the pavement. Being in a room full of people who are looking at you and laughing hysterically. Realizing your dad's gonna be ticked when you arrive home and, he finds it looks and smells like a toilet because you didn't let the dog out. All of these have "unknown" in them! Is he going to drop me to my death? Are they laughing at me and why? Is the dog crapping on the couch or is he urinating on the arm of dad's chair again like the last time?

Let me say this and hopefully it makes sense to you. We are all alone within ourselves, you are alone and each of the hundred people laughing are alone within themselves. No one is ganging up on you in the convenience store and you shouldn't really care if they are. They don't walk in your shoes.

Scenario: I'm standing in line at the bank and realize my hair's a wreck, my socks don't match, I never washed my hands after finger painting class and I spilled Juicy-Juice down the front of my shirt earlier that morning. I can't get out of there fast enough, right? "Who cares?" What no one knows is that for three years I've been working on a nuclear fountain pen that will make me second-to-Thomas Edison, or I've got something happening so big that this time next year, I'll be living on the coast of Hawaii.

Do you see what I mean? People don't have a clue about you. You could be the greatest and most powerful person in America. Just because your socks don't match means nothing. Be comfortable with who you are. Besides there is always someone who has got it worse than you do and, chances are, they're standing right next to you in a new suit.

Story: A guy I knew was the owner of a gas and service station. I used to stop in and hangout from time to time. One day while I was in there, this lady comes in to talk to Ted. She was driving a Jaguar, wearing a nice long fur coat and had gold hanging off her everywhere. After she left, Ted said, "You would think she was as rich as anything by looking at her, but every time she pays me she uses a credit card. The other day, we went through like six cards before we found one that would cover the bill."

Just because they look better, doesn't mean squat. They could be in debt right up to their eyeballs.

Story: I was on a plane a number of years ago. I had the window seat with two guys sitting to the left of me. The plane had taken off and, after sitting in silence for a hour or so, I leaned forward to face the two gentlemen and asked, "So what do you guys do for a living?" They were both dressed in suits. The guy directly next to me said he was a salesman for some company and was quite friendly. He and I actually talked for quite a while. The other fella closest to the aisle had a <u>real</u> nice suit, his shirt was glowing white and starched stiff. He didn't have much to say, stuck his nose up and answered briefly as if to say he didn't want to be dragged into conversation with us low-class people and proceeded to ignore us like the plague.

The plane made its destination, taxied to the gate and when the seatbelt sign turned off everyone began to move about, retrieving their belongings from the overhead compartments. As Mr. Snobby in the aisle seat reached up for his things I noticed a huge, deep brown, coffee stain running down the front of his glowing white shirt. A few things ran through my head (we won't get into them) but I kept my eye on him until he glanced down and noticed for himself, the horrible monster.

The first thing he did after his eyes popped out, was to look around quick and (I assumed) see if anyone was laughing at him. Then he tried, very unsuccessfully to cover it with his tie. At this point, I'm sure his day was destroyed. Why? Maybe he was mistaken and thought he was the only one that's ever happened to or maybe he thought that he was the best and that sort of thing should never happen to a man of his caliber?? Either way, anxiety was in the near future, I'm sure. Dude, forget the stain, deal with it when you can and don't let it eat you alive. I can hear News Nine now... "Man attacked himself today on flight 121, foaming at the mouth, violently ripping the shirt off his back, throwing himself to the floor and was removed by men in white suits." Get over it, get on with it. Who cares what people think because most people's opinions are just about worthless anyways. Don't let the fear of what someone else thinks rule you! First of all, you have no idea what they're thinking and who cares anyway.

Different topic: You have heard, "You are what you eat." Well, it does have some truth to it, if you use it hypothetically. I'll use it this way... what you listen to and dwell on can change your attitude and ultimately form who you are.

Years ago, I worked at a mill stacking lumber. If you have ever worked in a New Hampshire saw mill you would have a good idea of what I'm talking about. If you haven't I'll try to paint the picture of it all in your mind.

The cutting operation with the saws and

stuff are in a big building. The boards are cut and then ride a chain conveyor to the people (stackers) who stack the lumber outside. The one particular mill I'm talking about in this story had a trough about ten feet above the ground. The boards ride in the troth until they hit a stopper that's set at a certain width. The the boards then fall down into a bin with boards of the same width, no matter the length. The stackers then remove the boards from the bins and neatly put them in piles, called packs.

   There are five to ten stackers and usually the guys will pair up. If there are long boards in the bins, it will be easier to handle them from each end. After working there for quite some time, one would get to know all the guys at least a little bit... if you're anything like me.

   In this mill the boards fell out of the trough and down into the bins on two sides. This particular day I only worked one side, once in a while going to the other side for one reason or another. There was a guy named Chad working on the other side, whom I got along with quite well. He was wearing earphones as did a lot of guys and he was in fair spirits most of the day. Just after noon, I was going to use the bathroom and had to walk by the other side. As I approached Chad, I noticed he had a bad scowl on his face and looked real ticked off. I stopped and asked him what was wrong. He pulled an earphone away from his head long enough for me to repeat myself, then he gave me a horrible look like maybe he wanted to kill me and snapped, "Nothin!" I took that as, "Get out of my face... Now!" As I continued on my way to the outhouse, I was thinking about the encounter. Suddenly something dawned on me and on my way back through, I stopped again and this time I asked him what he was listening to. Again he pulled a headphone away long enough for me to repeat myself and then growled, "Manson". I knew it! It was the earphones and whatever it was he was listening to that brought on the nasty mood. Some music can lift you up and some can drag you down.

Glen told me one time, "Every time we listen to Zombie the cops come, it's like a cloud forms over the house."

James told me, "I love Dave Mathews, but I can only listen to so much, because it makes me depressed."

I went and saw Pantera in the Boston Orphium and got punched in the face like so many others. I saw four stretchers go through the crowd that night. The whole place turned into the combat zone.

What we listen to can definitely affect our attitudes and ultimately who we are, or what we become.

Not only music, but a topic of conversation can really set people off as well. I not only stay away from some music, but also too much news, politics (to a degree) and certain conversations, like on the condition of the world. I think it's good to be aware of what's happening, but it can also be overwhelming if you start meditating on the end of the world. I believe we all as citizens have a duty to vote, but when I'm hearing all kinds of horrible things, I have to shut it off. Why? I know when things aren't right just like the next guy, but to dwell on things I haven't any control over, wastes time, energy, emotions... and whatever else you involve. One can only do what they know to do in situations beyond your control and then hope for the best. I don't stick my head in the sand about it, but I don't lose a bunch of sleep over it either. I can't be sure what's going to happen tomorrow, neither can you and, believe it or not, neither does the news media. So, I want to stay as positive as I can about it all and pray it works out. We can always hope for the best!

Hey, you do what you want. I'm just making a couple of suggestions. I don't claim to have it all going on but I am going to work for it. Choose for life to be a constant progression. If you aren't exactly happy with who you are or what you are becoming, maybe you should consider what it is your putting in, what you've been chewing on so to speak-that may mean television also. Good grief, some wacko out in Hollywood comes up with an off-the-wall idea that little blue men are living inside us and then preaches it to the world. Ninety-eight percent of America watches it on television, fifty percent are thinking about it and another twenty percent actually think it's the truth.

I don't know about you, but I want to win this thing. When it come to life I believe there are winners and there are losers. A winner would be someone who is satisfied in the end and did the best he/she could during the process. The Good Book says, "Be careful how you hear." I believe every ear needs a bouncer at the door to bounce the crap that discourages us and brings us down, ultimately throwing us off course.

Hoping for the best is optimism... We should always strive to be an optimist. Like I said, you do what you want because you can and you will. But it's a decision, **always** with the option you can change your mind at anytime. You are the only one that can.

I used to always expect the worst of everything with the mindset that if it didn't happen, I was doing good and if it did happen, I wouldn't be let down. But as I go through life and see differently along the way I have realized: thinking like that brings me down. What I need to do is hope for the best and if I get let down, hope for the best again.

I have done a significant amount of hiking in my time and I do know that if you don't put one foot in front of the other, you won't make it to the beautiful view of the mountain range and have a breathtaking lunch. You can kick rocks around all day, complaining about the steep inclines and how long it's going to take, but if you don't get going the sun will go down and you'll miss it all. Don't waste time, start moving yourself into optimism. I once heard a guy say, "Time is our most valuable commodity." He's right! We only get one life and one shot at it, with only so much time.

The fact is that you and bad decisions are the only thing holding you back from greatness! I heard another man say, he wakes up every morning and looks at his worst enemy in the mirror. It's true, we are our worst enemy. Why? Because no one is to blame but ourselves, but that doesn't mean kick yourself around. It means accept responsibility, take one on the chin, get up, press on and try not to make the same mistakes over again. The Good Book says, "This one thing I do, is forget what lies behind and press on".

FOOD FOR THOUGHT

Here's a few things to think about: Is the wheel the best way to travel? It seemed the most reasonable at the time it was invented, but what about now? Gears and things have been useful over the years, but are there other ways with what is available to us today? In other words: The only things that aren't in existence, haven't been thought of yet. Who's going to think of them and put them into action? Could be you, but they won't go anywhere unless you do something about it. Finding out how to do this may not be the easiest, but you'll have to go through the steps like everyone else that makes it somewhere if you want it bad enough.

You will have to use persistence and determination and I can guarantee you won't do it sitting on the couch, playing PS3 and watching reality shows. It will get done by putting your nose to the grind and continually moving forward... pressing on.

As time passes me by, I get more and more determined to do something productive with it. That's what it's going to take to access what it is you see for yourself.

I was in a court room not too long ago, listening to motions and watching the lawyers hash it out, while the judge was intently asked questions. I thought to myself, "Geez, I could do this-basically put up an argument using the facts and some opinions. A good fight with words... Easy enough, who can't argue?" Same thing with a doctor- knowing where to cut and how far to go. Anyone with classes and practice could do either of these. The point is, anybody could do this stuff with time and money for school, and many people work their way through collage. You don't necessarily have to go to a full time school either. A lot of people do classes at a community college. At least start something in the direction you're thinking you want to go. You could even get a good jump on it by reading stuff on the Internet.

I heard a guy say one time, "The only way to get where you want to be is by leaving where you're at." Everyone can leave... in your mind! In your mind you can go anywhere and do anything and it's in your mind where it all begins. A dream or a vision, paint a picture in your mind of the way you want things to be and then press on.

Worst case scenarios: There is always the worst case and I think everyone should be aware of it in whatever it is they're doing. In other words, what's the worst thing that can happen-because it can and it may. I'm not saying you should be afraid, because you shouldn't. I'm saying realize the consequences of the risks you take. I can guarantee some are not worth it.

I know a girl (whose name won't be mentioned) who got pregnant the first time she ever had sex. As far as I know the child never even saw her father. PS: I don't believe it's totally his fault either.

I read this story in a newspaper many years ago and the incident took place one town away on Maple street. Three teenage kids were drinking all night, the driver was showing off, he lost control of the vehicle and hit a big oak tree. A seventeen year old dude riding in the backseat was squeezed between the door that got crushed in on him and a near empty keg of beer, killing him by suffocation.

I already told you the story of the kid doing cocaine for the first time. If you're not familiar with it, you should read the book again- which probably wouldn't be a bad idea and it would keep you busy for a few more hours. [Smile]

I also know a guy in his fifties who had his eye shot out by his brother's BB gun. He had a glass eye which may sound cool, but he can't see out of it.

The Good Book says: For what is your life? It is even a vapor that appears for a little time and then vanishes away.

Let's do the right thing while we still have one.

GOD

This is the most important chapter in this book. We definitely saved the best for last.

First of all, you believe what you want, no one will make you do anything when it comes to your faith. It's all you! This is what I believe and I'm entitled to my beliefs as well as the next guy.

I will first discuss the most printed book in the world called the Holy Bible and will try to sum it up using my words, for those of you who don't know much about it.

The word Bible has a lesser meaning and here is the definition from **Webster's**: #4. A reference publication esteemed for its usefulness and authority. Many cars and trucks have bibles for them. It's a handbook that contains every piece, every part from bumper to bumper, where and how it fits. In the back of these books there is even a wire diagram to show where each and every little wire goes. It also has a trouble shooting section describing problems the vehicle may have and some solutions to try and correct them. Basically, everything you need to know right down to which spark plug fires first is between the covers of the vehicle's bible.

The Holy Bible I believe is the handbook to life. It's a book made up of

many books and letters to those who believe. The first "book" in the Bible is Genesis, the book of beginnings. The second is Exodus, this is the one with Moses in it. The fourth book is boring to most people, but it is a book of genealogy called Numbers. These three books are part of the old testament. Some of the books in the Old Testament were written by prophets, priests and kings, but all were people who believed in the same God.

The New Testament is made up from eye witness reports about the man Jesus and mostly letters from a guy named Paul to different churches and people who believed. It ends with Revelations, which is about visions given to and recorded by a man named John.

The Bible is actually a bloody book of love written, composed and kept to inform people of a certain God and truths about life. Some people say there is only one God but I disagree...
Webster's def. God: #3. Any deified person or object.

I believe humans have all kinds of gods, whatever they may be. Think about the rabbit's foot, no one is counting on the rabbit's cut off foot to hop away and bring back greatness. So, what is it? It's something behind the foot, something we can't see. Money makes an easy god, and why not? People kill for it everyday. Ever see anyone pray to luck? Rubbing on the coin, crossing the fingers.

The Holy Bible even talks of many gods, however it does say, "There is only one true, <u>living</u> God." He was the God of Abraham, Issac and Jacob-who were three men who lived a long time ago and were said by their neighbors to have served a great and powerful God.

The Old Testament was written by Jews, because they were the nation serving the living God at the time. Then Jesus preached, "Not only for the Jew but for the gentile" and began the New Testament. Same God! The New Testament was written mostly in Greek.

The people who believe and follow the Bible, particularly the New Testament, are called Christians or people who follow Christ. By the way, Christ isn't a last name. It actually means the chosen one of God, Saviour, or Messiah. The whole Bible is actually about the Christ whose name is Jesus and He was from a town called Nazareth, which is why you may have heard "Jesus of Nazareth". Back a couple thousand years ago when there weren't as many people, last names weren't that necessary. Many people were called by their name, followed by a little description. For instance, if your name was Rick and your father was Sam, they may have called you "Rick, son of Sam". So after Jesus death people remembered Him as the Christ. To this day, He is Jesus Christ. Funny, how many times have you heard "Jesus Christ" and even said it yourself?

Anyway, I have heard many people say over the years, "I tried to read the Bible but it lost me." I can guess they got lost around the third or fourth book, probably the one called Leviticus or Numbers. These particular books would lose most anyone unless you have been in the Bible a while.

I would usually tell someone to start in the New Testament with a book called John. It may sound strange to start reading a book more than half way through it, but it does make sense in this case-unless you are a Jew, and/or know the customs and laws of the Jews.

The first books of the New Testament are Mathew, Mark, Luke and John. They are the eyewitness reports of Jesus' works and teachings-also called the Gospels (which means Good News).

The book of Acts is about the Spirit of God and how a man who was butchering Christians was converted by the power of God. The book of Romans was a letter written to new Christians in Rome. Followed by many other letters (Galatians, Ephesians, Philippians...) written to Christians in different churches.

The original languages of the Bible were translated into Latin around 1455. Then at the end of the Dark Ages in 1611, a great king of England named James listened to the scriptures at a monastery,

where the Bible was kept under lock and key and only to be read by monks. He put faith in what he heard and then he ordered the scriptures translated from the original Greek and Hebrew into the English language, mass printed and distributed everywhere. That translation of the Bible was later named "The King James Version" and used in thousands of churches today. Over the last fifty or so years, people have come up with other versions like the New King James, New American Standard and the NIV (New International Version). They wrote them to make it easier to read, changing Elizabethan words like thou and thy, into words like you and your, but the doctrine of these three versions stayed the same. In other words, they tell the same story without the Archaic lingo.

The God of the Holy Bible is Love, Light, Life, Peace, Hope, the Comforter, Mercy... the God of more than enough and the list goes on. I guess you would have to read for yourself to find all the words used to describe Him.

The settlers of this continent believed in Him and wrote stories about His greatness. Thanksgiving is a story of the petition for rain answered by God. The founders of this nation trusted Him and put their faith on the currency, declared Him in the saluting of the flag and held Him in esteem in the Declaration of Independence and even atop the Washington monument. The Bible says He is, He was and always will be. He is the first, the last, the Alpha and the Omega. **BUT** when it comes to God the Good Book says, "By faith" you will see. By faith, we will move God. "But let him ask in faith without any doubting, he who doubts is like a wave of the sea driven with the wind and tossed, let not that man think he will receive anything from God." James 1:6-7

If you muster faith, round it up and chose to believe, you will see God. Not with your eyes, but within you and all around you. You will have peace and know that He is who He said He is and you will also witness His power. I can't convince you, no one but He can do that. Again, you are the only one who will ultimately make the decision to turn on the power of God in your life. If you seek, you will find. If you knock the door will be open. The Book says it, I believe it and now I know it!

I read the Bible, I talk to God, I go to church and listen to people who have chosen to serve Him. I believe what the Bible says. It's a choice I made and I'm glad I did.

Story: One morning about five years ago, at about 7:30 in the morning, I was up and getting ready for work when the telephone was ringing in the next room. My wife answered the phone as I was on my way down the stairs, then she hollered to me, "Did you call Pennsylvania?"

"What?" I said "Did you call Pennsylvania this morning?" she asked again. I told her I hadn't called anyone that morning and out the door I went. I got in my truck with another guy who met me at my house in the mornings and we headed out to Home Depot. My phone rang when we got into the parking lot. It was my wife and she said, "That was weird. The lady on the phone was in Philadelphia, PA and the reason she was calling was because our phone number showed up on her caller ID. She didn't get to the phone quick enough and was calling us back." The lady asked where we lived, my wife told her what state and town we were in. Then the lady said, "That's weird, my nephew is in jail there."

Gears started turning in my head when she said that to me... I was asking myself, "Why and how would my number show up on her called ID?" She has a nephew in jail, the same jail I have been going into and talking with guys for about ten years. All I could think was that somehow an inmate billed my number for a call elsewhere, but how would my number actually appear on her Caller ID?? That's digital, isn't it? Maybe they figured out a combination of digits or some weird way of... somehow doing it??? The other problem I was having with it, was that I never ever gave out my number to inmates. So who would know or be able to do this?? I called my wife back and asked what the lady's name was and for her phone number and then I called the number. What sounded like an elderly black woman answered the phone. I told her I was the guy whose house she had just called. She said to me, "Sir, I'm sorry. I have cataracts on my eyes real bad and I misread the number. The number on the caller ID was 555-542-9125." The five... it was the five at the end, mine was a nine. I talked to her for a few minutes, long enough to learn she was a Methodist and she's been praying for this guy in jail for many years. He was a 62-year-old black guy, over six feet tall. "He is sneaky," she said. He's in jail for identity theft and was in all kinds of trouble. After we hung up, I looked at the guy sitting next to me in the truck and said "That was weird." I told him the story... thus far.

Think: A elderly Methodist lady misreads her Caller ID by one number. She contacts a guy who visits the same jail her nephew is in from halfway across the country-one of five guys that visit and talk about the same God she has been praying to all these years. Trriiiiip!

I called the number she gave me and it was the number to the pay-phone at the jail. The recording said something like this, "I'm sorry, but the number you dialed does not receive calls".

Problem: How many numbers are we working with here? Ten numbers, one wrong and she got me. She could only get one wrong for it to be me-the last number and it had to be a nine instead of a five.

Somebody think about it and do the math. I'm not sure I could figure out this problem, but I wouldn't mind knowing the answer or even if there was one.

I've thought about this problem a thousand times. I believe she had a combination of nine-hundred and ninety numbers. If she messed up any of the first three numbers she would have got a different state. If she messed up the fourth or fifth number she would have gotten a different town. Anyone of the last five numbers and she would have at least gotten the same community, but then factor in the number of people who actually visit this jail to the number of people in the community. Another problem within the problem, what are the odds of my number being one number off from the pay-phone in the jail, which was actually the number she was trying to call back. Somehow there has to be an answer, but I think one would have to be a mathematical genius to come up with it. Anyway, I was then armed with his name and description. Knowing a few of the other guys that go to the same jail and one of them happening to go the same church as I did, I told him the story about the phone call. A couple of days later he handed me a newspaper clipping. It was about this guy in jail, he is sneaky. He has been arrested all over the place and wanted in a few other states as well for writing bad checks with a total in excess of three million dollars. (No misprint.) Three million dollars. Crazy huh? I thought so. I guess one of the checks was to a coffee company in Columbia for almost a million dollars and the rest were spread out all over the place.

A few weeks later I was able to get up to the jail. The guard told me that only a couple of guys had come out to visit and that there was a fellow in there talking with them in the library. He told me if I wanted to go in that was fine. Then I broke one of my own rules: I never asked for a certain person. If they want to talk, they'll come out. If not, leave them be. Well, I asked for this particular fella. The guard said he would go and ask if he wanted to visit with me. He then came back and said the man would visit with me, brought me into a small room and told me that he would go get him and bring him out. Finally they arrived, I stood up to introduce myself, shook his hand and invited him to sit down. The man sat down and then I asked him, "Do you believe in divine appointment?" Looking quite skeptical, he leaned back in his chair, folded his arms and motioned his head up and down slowly, as if reluctantly saying yes.

Then I told him the story in detail of the phone call I'd received a month ago, where it was from and I noticed as I said the lady's name he mouthed it at the same time. I think it was then that I had his full attention. He sat forward, placed his elbows on his knees and listened intently to what I had to say, adding bits/pieces here and there. In the three hours we talked, I learned that we had both hung out on Washington Heights ("It ain't right being white on the heights") in New York City, we'd both been through the 34th ("Dirty-Fourth") precinct in Manhattan.

zWe had both lived in DelCab county GA. It was strange. We had so much in common, it was crazy. However, he was far more knowledgeable than I and had studied many religions, gods and books. It was ridiculous how much he knew. Finally at one point, I said to God under my breath, "You'll have to do something here, say what you want. You'll have to be the one who talks to this guy because he's too smart for me. I can't compete with this." A few minutes later I showed him a few verses in Romans and when I looked up at him, he was staring at me like a deer in the headlights. "That's it!" he said. "What?" I asked. "That's it!" he said again, still giving me the deer look. "What's it?" I asked again. "Faith" he answered. "It's all about faith, isn't it?" The Word of God hit him right between the eyes.

Before we were done talking, he told me his side of the story. He kind of wound up in this small town because he was visiting his girlfriend's brother (or something like that) and was only suppose to be here a few days. While he was here, he went to Walmart picked out a computer and some gift cards worth a couple thousand bucks. He went to the register with the stuff and wrote a check, posing as a doctor. He said everything went smooth and he left the store. Then he got hung up for a few more days and decided to go back and do it again. "I broke my own rule," he said. "I never go back to the same place twice." Again he got a computer, more gift cards and went to the register. Again everything went smooth and he left the store. Again he got hung up for a few more days and a third time he decided to go back to same store and do the same thing.

This time he said, "When I got to register and handed the lady the check, there was a problem and she had to call the manager over." He said, "Man, I knew I needed to just forget all about it and walk right out. I've been doing this a long time, I know the rules," he said. "But I stood there like an idiot. Then the manager told me everything was alright but it was going to take a few minutes to clear up the problem." He said "I knew what was going on and I knew if I wanted to get away, I should walk out the door right then but still I stood there and waited." He said, "After standing there like five minutes, I watched a cop walk in the door. I knew what he was doing there and I knew the whole time I was waiting there to be arrested but it was like I couldn't move... And now, talking to you, I know why I was standing there, because I was supposed to see you and hear what you had to say."

Then he told me this "I've been in many jails, but I don't stay because they kick me out. I know how to get out of jail (it's not a good idea to tell you what his methods were, so I'll leave that part out), but I'm done," he said. "I'm done getting out, I'm going to do my time. I'm changing up and going to do something with my life." I really believe he saw some things that night and made a change. He wrote me a couple of letters and the last I knew he was locked up in Tennessee.

God answered his aunt's prayers and worked a miracle on that man. In turn he chose to believe it was God and decided he was going to live a different life, which I'm sure was a good choice.

God doesn't need to be argued for, if you really want to know He'll get you there. Find out, life's too short not to. The Bible is the place to find the answers, read carefully the part called John (in between Luke and Acts) and ask God to help you understand what you're reading. He will help you and show up for you, just like He has millions of others.

(The Beginning)

For copies of this book
send $10.00/ea plus $2 S/H to the address below:

Enoch Hartwell
P.O. Box 955
Claremont, NH 03743

or pay through PayPal to the below e-address
wmwiswear@gmail.com
E-address also for correspondence
Ask about quantity discounts

Keep your eyes peeled for part two

"Whack me when I swear again"

CPSIA information can be obtained at www.ICGtesting.com
263896BV00002B/6/P